PRAISE FOR
Ellen Dugan

The Enchanted Cat
2007 COVR AWARD WINNER
Best Book Magick/Shamanism Category

Cottage Witchery
"This is the perfect book to have around
if you want to make every area of your
home magical."—*NewWitch*

Herb Magic for Beginners
"A delightful little book."—*Herb Quarterly*

Garden Witch's Herbal
"A refreshing change from other garden-
variety horticulture books…entertaining as
well as informative."—*New Age Retailer*

Elements of Witchcraft

"[Dugan's] wise-woman tone and gentle guidance will help nurture budding natural witches, and her well-written text will guide novices in their discoveries as well."—*School Library Journal*

Natural Witchery

2008 COVR AWARD WINNER
Best Book Wicca/Paganism Category

"Interspersed throughout the text are lively anecdotes from Dugan's own Samantha Stephens–esque household. The value of this book lies in the warm, personal touch Dugan uses both in her writing and in her craft."—*Publishers Weekly*

"This book is eminently useful. Dugan's voice is engaging and her work is practical and fun."—*PanGaia*

"A gold mine of concepts and resources for the novice to intermediate practitioner… Chock-full of relevant wisdom and lively humor."—*Library Journal*

The *Natural* PSYCHIC

Ellen Dugan is an award-winning author and psychic-clairvoyant who has been a practicing Witch for thirty years. She is high priestess of a mixed magick tradition coven in the St. Louis area. She gardens and practices her Craft in Missouri, where she lives with her family. Also known as the Garden Witch, she is the author of many Llewellyn books, including *Garden Witchery*, *Cottage Witchery*, *Natural Witchery*, and *Garden Witch's Herbal*. Ellen is also an experienced lecturer on a variety of topics, including tarot, psychometry, Witchcraft, and enchanted gardens.

The *Natural* PSYCHIC

Ellen Dugan's
Personal Guide to the Psychic Realm

LLEWELLYN PUBLICATIONS
Woodbury, Minnesota

FIRST EDITION
First Printing, 2015

Book design by Rebecca Zins
Cover design by Kevin R. Brown
Cover photo: Shutterstock/110065796/©Standret
Interior scroll background from *Flowers Vector Designs* (Dover Publications, 2010)

Llewellyn Publications is a registered trademark of Llewellyn Worldwide Ltd.

Library of Congress Cataloging-in-Publication Data
Dugan, Ellen, 1963–
The natural psychic : Ellen Dugan's personal guide to the psychic realm.
—First edition.
    pages cm
Includes bibliographical references and index.
ISBN 978-0-7387-4335-6
1. Psychic ability. I. Title.
BF1031.D93 2015
133.8—dc23

                                    2015002512

Llewellyn Publications
A Division of Llewellyn Worldwide Ltd.
2143 Wooddale Drive
Woodbury, MN 55125-2989
www.llewellyn.com

Printed in the United States of America

For my children
Kraig, Kyle, and Erin
and for my niece
Olivia
who all have their own gifts and psychic
abilities and who will one day pass these
talents along to the next generation.

Remember where you come from and what
I have taught you. Those very qualities that
make us different are what make us united and
stronger as a family. Honor the past, enjoy the
present, and embrace the future. Love you.

Contents

Chapter 6

Psychic Phenomena: Psi-Sensitives, Ghost Hunters, Séances & SLIders 97

Chapter 7

Psychic Training 113

Chapter 8

Psychic First Aid, Protection, and Self-Defense 127

Acknowledgments

To my husband, Ken, who patiently listened and helped me reorganize and eventually find my way through the maze. To Clyde for his honesty and perspective. Thanks to both Jeanne and Mitchell for the assist on martial arts terminology and for providing a different insight on self-defense. To Bonnie for reminding me at the eleventh hour to stretch and embrace the challenge. To Ember Grant for the on-the-spot crystal information.

Also with appreciation to Meme, Charlynn, Becca, Robbie, Tess Whitehurst, Kristoffer Hughes, and Christopher Penczak for their friendship and support.

A special thank you to my editors Angela Wix and Becky Zins, who were enthusiastic about this topic from the beginning. Ladies, you rock!

ONE OF THE *most courageous things*
you can do is to identify yourself:
know who you are, what you believe
in, and where you want to go.

Sheila Murray Bethel

THE KEY TO growth is the introduction of higher dimensions of consciousness into our awareness.

Lao Tzu

Introduction

I am a psychic. I am pretty confident that you are too! Even if you haven't fully discovered or developed your abilities, the fact that you picked up this book says something about your desire and capabilities for learning more. I am here to help you explore the psychic realm and learn skills that will help you in many ways.

Let's begin by clearing up a big old inaccurate psychic belief. Since you will probably pick up on this throughout the rest of the book, I would like to clarify up front that in addition to being a psychic, I am also a

Witch. However, this belief system has no direct impact on the training I am providing here. Perhaps you are a Judeo-Christian, Agnostic, Atheist, Spiritualist, Wiccan, Witch, or Pagan seeking some information. Maybe you are into angels or you see the Divine in everything and are of a more mystical bent; well, that's fantastic. Believe what brings you inspiration and support in life, but also know that religious affiliations have nothing to do with psychic potential. Psychic abilities don't work because you have a certain belief; they work because they are a part of our makeup— they are a skill.

I am going to repeat myself again because it is so important to me that you understand this fact: *psychic ability has nothing to do with religion, nor does practicing a certain type of religion make you a more talented psychic.* Surprise! Certainly your religious practices may flavor your psychic work; however, it does not influence individual psychic talents. You are who you are. How you choose to connect and interact with the Divine is strictly up to you. Your psychic abilities and talents are yours to explore no matter what your religious affiliation.

This is the #1 misunderstanding that I have come up against repeatedly over the years, and it often hinders development through the fear that holds us back in various ways. I would never say, "Hey, this psychic stuff works for me because I am a Witch." That is simply not true. Our religious beliefs are our own personal business and have no impact on our psychic development, so let's break free of that inaccurate notion. Learn these skills for empowerment and growth no matter what your religious beliefs may be.

How I Came to Write This Book

The idea for this book simmered away on the back burner of my mind for several years. It has always been frustrating for me to search for books on psychic abilities: all I want is some solid, straight information, but I have to wade through beliefs that are not in line with my own and have no real influence in the realm of psychic development. It's like the author is compelled to tell you that you shouldn't be afraid to read about this topic because they have this or that higher power or knowledge on their side. Something was off about this approach to me, and I knew I couldn't be alone. I wanted to offer something for other readers like me who were searching for a nondenominational approach to psychic development.

I would occasionally take out the outline and refine it, tinker with it for a few days, and add a bit of this and a touch of that. Ideas would shift around, and eventually the book would let me know that it wasn't quite ready. So I tucked it away and worked on my other book projects. It never felt like the right time to push forward with this topic, and as I am good with hunches and listening to my instincts, I let it be.

It was after I finished up my fifteenth book that I finally took a break. I took a few months off and traveled around doing author events and lectures. These lectures often sidelined into discussing psychic abilities, and that's when the interesting questions about the topic really began. More and more I could feel the need for this book, and when my events slowed down and I had the whole summer before me, I acted on the nudge to begin the writing process. Interestingly, the day I pitched this book to my publisher I received an incredible amount of psychic-themed questions at an event. That was my official cue! It was time.

Experience: Here Is How I Gained Mine

You may be wondering *who is this woman anyway and why should I listen to her on the topic of psychic abilities?* I am a psychic-clairvoyant, meaning I can psychically see, meaning I can see the past, present, and future. I am clairtangent, which means I can use psychic touch to read people and objects. I am clairsentient, also known as an empathic, meaning I can psychically sense and feel the emotions of others. I'm claircognizant, which is the formal term for a psychic intuitive—an individual who has an immediate insight or cognition—and finally I am a medium too. You *betcha* I have street cred—and let me tell you I have earned it. I have been performing clairvoyant readings professionally for over twenty-five years. But I did not just wake up one morning to be—*ta-da!*—an instant professional psychic. I have had decades of life experience as a psychic. However, it took time, perseverance, and a lot of work to get to where I am today.

As a child I could see and sense things that other people could not, and I often blurted out what I saw or felt. "Great Uncle has a bad heart," I once announced while I sat on the lap of the relative in question. When he suddenly passed away a few months later from an undiagnosed heart condition, my parents were not amused.

I figured out early on that what I was seeing and feeling was not seen or experienced by other people, nor was it understood or accepted by my family. My family was frightened and embarrassed by this, and so I was punished. Mostly I was punished for just being "different." Keep in mind that I was born in 1963; honestly, things were different back then. People didn't talk about psychic abilities, at least not in polite middle-class Midwestern conversation. It was considered somewhat scandalous.

I'm not sharing this information about my childhood for sympathy but to point out something important that may affect many of my readers. There is a theory that links a past of childhood physical abuse and traumatic experiences to stronger psychic ability in adults. When someone lives in a state of constant fear, their adrenalin is always pumping and they become hyperaware of the mood of a room and the emotions of the people closest to them.

Think about it: when you are frightened, adrenalin pumps through your system. You become more alert. That adrenalin rush can help you react faster, jump higher, or become stronger. It is an instinct and a way to ensure our survival as a species. Furthermore, this state of hyperawareness creates a sort of altered state where everything slows down, allowing your senses to heighten and consciousness to expand. Now imagine a child living like that every day for years at a time.

Children living in emotionally or physically abusive environments tend to develop a hypersensitivity to the moods and temperaments of the people around them. It's a survival skill. They do this so they are always on alert and hopefully can keep themselves out of the line of fire. I have seen this described as a sort of preternatural awareness. These psychically sensitive kids quickly learn to be constantly aware and to monitor the moods and emotions around them so they have a better chance of avoiding mistreatment.

There is also the speculation that children who are naturally gifted psychics just shine forth with a light, an energy, or a different sort of vibe, and it is this difference that, sadly, often attracts abuse. While I don't particularly care for that line of thought, it is true that sometimes the people who should nurture, protect, and love their children the most react to what they fear or cannot understand with emotional abuse or physical violence.

My family really hadn't bargained for an artsy, creative, sarcastic, and obviously psychic child. The last thing they were prepared to deal with was a kid who had a mystical bent. When punishment and attempts at emotional manipulation did not work, they switched to other tactics. For example, when I was a teenager, they hauled me off to a minister for counseling, thinking I needed a religious intervention.

I vividly recall sitting in the minister's office. He was a kind, soft-spoken man. I was pretty outraged at the situation. I was a good kid—I had average grades, I didn't smoke or drink, I didn't do drugs—but my reputation preceded me at the church because I asked questions that most wouldn't.

The minister and I chatted for a while, and then he gave me the speech I expected: "Your parents love you—they are only concerned..." I just glared at him and did not budge an inch. When he asked me to tell him about these visions I thought I had been experiencing, that really put my back up.

I was honest and told him flat-out what I could see, and I proved it by pulling things right out of his head. He jolted a couple of times at my accuracy. After a time, he gently suggested to me that perhaps he should speak to my family about taking me to see a doctor. Perhaps there was a medication I could take to stop my visions—so I could lead a normal life.

To which my indignant response was, "Hey, if I could play the piano amazingly well, and no one could understand or explain how I could do that, would you tell me to consider taking medication to stop playing music?"

I remember crossing my arms and arguing that there was nothing wrong with me at all; in fact, I said, *he* was looking at it the wrong way. I argued that some people were talented in music or art, some people might be gifted athletes, and maybe some people were naturally talented in other things.

The minister looked at me thoughtfully and then smiled. He chuckled and admitted that I had just made a very good point. After that, things improved for me at home somewhat, and I threw myself into research.

I hit the library and read everything I could get my little hands on about the topics of extrasensory perception (what they used to call ESP back in the day) and psychic abilities. Then I met a wonderful teacher when I was a high school senior. A known psychic, she was a popular teacher at my school and she helped me by suggesting books to read and other techniques that I could use to understand more of what I was experiencing. At her suggestion, I wrote a term paper on the subject of ESP, and I was so proud of that paper and the grade I received.

I was determined to learn more, so I studied in secret since the topic still upset my family, then practiced what I learned with friends. I made lots of new "friends" my senior year at high school when word got out that I was a psychic. However, I was so relieved that at last someone thought what I could do was cool, I really didn't mind. It was better than feeling alone. In desperation, I got involved in lots of school activities and stayed out of the house as much as possible. Basically, I survived.

I got engaged to a nice, open-minded young man the summer after I graduated from high school and was married the following spring. I continued to work on my psychic abilities and talents as a young bride and also while I raised our three children. When my children were small, I challenged myself by trying out for and then working the local psychic fairs as a reader.

Let me just say this about working big psychic fairs: if you want a crash course in being able to read for anybody, that'll pretty much do it. I quickly earned a reputation as being an accurate, down-to-earth, honest clairvoyant and tarot card reader.

As my kids hit their teens, my first book was published. When the kids finished high school, I became a full-time author. I have honed my psychic talents even more in the past twelve years while teaching and touring North America.

I was born with a capability or natural psychic aptitude, and my childhood environment shaped me into being more psychically alert. But it is persistence, practice, practical application, and hard work that has got me to where I am today.

As you begin working through this book, I suggest that you pick up a notebook and devote it to your personal psychic development. I want you to actually write down when you have a psychic experience. Date it, make notes, and then when the event plays out or you have confirmation that you were correct, note that down, too. Add your personal impressions as well, and be sure to mark the date when you received your confirmation about the event. In a few months you will look back at that notebook and start to see a pattern in your own abilities.

What may seem insignificant at the time will provide insight a few months later. This personal psychic record keeping takes patience and commitment. However, if you truly want solid confirmation as to exactly where your talents lie and how you correctly divine information, then you need to put in the work. When you track your psychic experiences, you will begin to notice patterns. When you notice patterns, you begin to understand how your personal abilities manifest. This provides validation, and validation is the key to learning more about your own talents.

Psychic Ability Is a Natural Talent or Skill

Psychic ability is a natural talent that is inherent in all of us—everyone has some type of psychic ability, but not everyone chooses to acknowledge or embrace it. It is true that some folks are able to access this natural talent easier than others or they just seem to have a knack for it, while other individuals have to work very hard to get any results at all.

The best explanation I can give you comes in the form of an analogy: everybody can sing…but some people are *singers*. So you might be able to carry a pleasant tune or maybe you are able to sing effortlessly in harmony along with songs on the radio. Perhaps you wow at karaoke or possibly you are more along the lines of a Broadway singing sensation.

There are some folks who come into this world with the ability to perceive things that many people cannot. They are born psychically sensitive. Others may have to walk a hard road and turn those abilities into a preternatural skill in order to survive with a minimum of emotional or physical harm. But everyone has some type of natural psychic talent.

People love to say that psychic talent (or any talent, for that matter) is actually a gift, which makes lots of folks think, "Oh, as in gifts from God?" That depends on how you look at it. Again, your religious affiliation honestly has nothing to do with whether or not you can access those natural abilities. Because—say it with me one more time—psychic ability is an aptitude or a skill.

Psychic ability can also be a hereditary ability. Yes, it does run in families. But I still have to point out that no matter how these psychic abilities manifested or came about, the individuals who hold them still have to refine that skill or talent. They will have to build on it and work with it to mold their talent into the best possible shape if they want to be successful, and that takes training, practice, and work.

When it comes to developing your psychic skill level, I suggest that you think of this like mental muscles. If you want to build them up, then you are going to have to start training. So the question is, are you ready to get to work?

It took courage, time, perseverance, and a lot of hard work to get to where I am today in regard to my psychic abilities. If it helps, think of me as your personal trainer when it comes to the use and practice of psychic abilities. Best of all, I have the information and experience that you need to understand and accomplish the goals you have set out for yourself as you explore your psychic talents. You will learn. You will laugh, and you will grow.

Let's warm up and start flexing those psychic muscles by taking a look at psychic experiences, or what I like to call the three Ps. They are premonition, precognition, and postcognition.

Chapter 1

Psychic Experiences

To begin, we will look at the terminology used to describe and classify psychic phenomena. This is important to tackle right at the beginning so you understand the difference between psychic experiences and psychic abilities. Once we get the vocabulary set, then we can move forward with clarity.

> **Psychic:** A person who is sensitive to nonphysical forces and influences and who obtains knowledge from outside the realm of the physical senses.

Experience: The process or fact of personally observing, encountering, or undergoing something.

Psychic experience: The process of personally experiencing or having a premonition, precognition, or postcognition.

Psychic ability: An individual's capability to receive information in a way that is beyond the nonphysical senses. This natural skill or aptitude is considered "extra"—as in extrasensory perception, or ESP for short.

In my opinion, psychic experiences should be explained before anything else. Without first having a psychic experience, you cannot understand your individual psychic ability or talent and how it manifests for you personally.

When it comes to psychic experiences, it is all about the personal experience—*your* personal experience. What you encounter, feel, or observe is of the utmost importance. The very fact that you have gone through the psychic experience or process is what is essential to comprehend and validate.

I classify psychic experiences as premonition, precognition, and postcognition (the three Ps). These psychic experiences give us the foundation that we need to understand and successfully work with all our natural psychic talents.

The Three Ps of Psychic Experiences

You have probably heard of premonition and precognition, but postcognition may be a new term for you. Honestly, premonition and precognition are misrepresented and incorrectly identified so often that it can make even a seasoned researcher a little twitchy. Premonition and precognition are often confusing for people, but they are two vastly different experiences. In an effort to clear this up once and for all, read the following information carefully and take your time:

Premonition: A premonition is an unclear forewarning accompanied by a simultaneous emotional reaction. This vague feeling of unease that something is wrong can be hard to pin down or put a name on. With a premonition you *feel* a sense of danger, urgency, or apprehension, but you do not receive any specific information; instead, this is all about that emotional feeling.

Precognition: Precognition, on the other hand, is the direct knowledge of events that have yet to occur. Precognition may be experienced in the dream state (as in precognitive dreams) or as a waking vision. However, precognition occurs with calmer, almost detached feelings. Precognition is very specific psychic information without any emotional reaction at the time the knowledge is received, such as "the missing wedding rings will be found inside of an old prescription bottle in Grandma's bathroom medicine chest." Precognition is all about data and distinct, detailed information.

The fastest way to remember which is which is to notice that at the beginning of the word premonition is *emo*, which is short for emotion. This tip is an easy way to differentiate the two, as premonitions are primarily emotional experiences.

A premonition always starts out as an unexpected emotional response that makes you wonder why you are suddenly feeling a certain way. It is all about that visceral emotional reaction, sometimes called a foreboding. When it comes to premonitions, you feel it first—then you wonder what is wrong.

This is worth repeating so you have the terminology down cold. If you experience a foreboding feeling accompanied simultaneously by an emotional reaction, that is a premonition. On the other hand, if you know *exactly* what is about to occur and have detailed information, then that is classified as precognition.

Premonition

A premonition is classically defined as an emotional forewarning. In layman's terms, it is that feeling that something, somewhere, is wrong. This feeling may be very hard to put a name to; some people may try to describe it as an apprehension or a sense of imminent danger. This intense emotional reaction is much more powerful than when folks say "I have a bad feeling about this..." Imagine that turned up to an gut-wrenching volume: your heart races, your belly tightens, and you are compelled to figure out what is wrong—right *now*.

Premonition is what makes mothers go check on their babies just in the nick of time. Premonition is what causes lifeguards look at a certain area of the pool at just the right moment so they can dive in and rescue a swimmer before it is too late. Premonition is the uneasy feeling that compels people to drive home by alternate routes, only to later discover that they have avoided a major accident.

A premonition is a foreboding feeling that, if paid attention to and followed through on, can allow us to be there when we are most needed. It can grant us enough time to possibly rescue another, or it may even give us the chance to change an unpleasant outcome by altering our behavior or plans.

Premonitions are powerful, as they grab hold of our attention by seizing our emotions and not letting up until we figure them out. With a premonition, the feeling that something is wrong is so intense that it cannot be ignored, which leads us to the next logical question: How in the world do we figure out exactly what's wrong?

Easy. Start asking yourself questions to get to the bottom of the premonition.

SUCCESSFULLY SOLVING THE MYSTERIOUS PREMONITION

Premonitions are feared because they seem so mysterious, and the element of the unknown frightens many of us. But instead of panicking during a premonition, use the power of your emotional response and channel it into something constructive. If you feel compelled to move, check on the little ones, or whatever requires you to move right then—such as changing lanes while driving or going home by a different route—well, then, by all means do it!

If you don't have the compulsion to move immediately, then visualize that rush of emotion and what is often referred to as the "fight or flight" response and put them to use instead. I visualize that intense emotional reaction as energy swirling around me. In my mind's eye I quickly reach out with my hands and gather up all of that nervous energy with both hands. (If I am alone, I may pantomime the action.) After I have a grip on it, I pull that feeling—that emotional reaction the premonition gave me—straight into my solar plexus, and I don't let go until I have the answers I am looking for.

Once you have that energy pulled close, stop and ask yourself some quick questions to get to the bottom of that foreboding feeling. Rattle off your questions silently to yourself—in your mind—to quickly get to the bottom of the premonition.

I figured out how to do this as a teenager, and honestly I just assumed that everyone did this technique. It wasn't until many years later—when I was lecturing on premonitions and answering a woman's question, explaining to her how simple it was to get to the bottom of them—that I watched with amazement as about seventy-five people jolted upright in their chairs and scrambled for notebooks to write down this information.

That was when I realized that this was *not* something everybody else did, but it really is easy. You will know you are on the right track to solving the premonition by the physical sensations your body gives you. Here is how I do it.

Putting the Premonition to Work

When I receive a premonition, I stop, take a deep breath, and then visualize that intense emotional reaction as energy swirling around me. As stated before, in my mind's eye I quickly reach out and gather up all of that nervous energy with both hands. After I grab it, I pull that feeling/emotional reaction the premonition gave me straight into my solar plexus.

(The solar plexus is located below the ribs and above the navel.) Then I start silently asking myself what I call preliminary questions, such as:

- Am I in danger?

- Is someone I love in danger?

- Which of my loved ones is in danger?
  (List them off quickly in your head.)

- Do I need to go somewhere or do something?

If I get a hit—a physical reaction such as my stomach or chest tightening—to one of my preliminary questions, then I follow that up by asking more specific questions. I call these my follow-up, or secondary, questions:

- Is the danger above me, below me, in front of
  me, behind me, to my right, or to my left?

- Is the danger above [my loved one], below them, in front
  of them, behind them, to their right, or to their left?

- Is so-and-so in trouble?

- Do they need help?

- Are they hurt?

- Are they sick?

- Are they upset?

Whatever question gives me the strongest physical response, or "hit" as I like to call it, helps me to quickly narrow the premonition down into more specific information that I can actually use. The process is fast; it maybe takes me ten seconds max. It may take you a bit longer when you begin, but it should not take you more than a minute.

You are going to have to work quickly—when the premonition is hot, in other words. Your best chance to obtain a good lead or gather solid information out of that premonition comes when emotions are at their peak.

PREMONITION: A REAL-LIFE APPLICATION

Here is a real-life example that will help explain the process. This past winter I had just come back from working out at the gym with my trainer and was standing in my kitchen sweating and guzzling the last of my water. I was thinking about how fabulous a nice hot shower sounded for my aching muscles, and as I turned to head down the hall, I had a premonition that something was wrong—and it was strong enough to stop me in my tracks.

I set down the now-empty water bottle and reached out with both hands (as I was alone in the house at the time). I pulled that foreboding feeling in tighter to my solar plexus and let that feeling of dread roll over me. In essence, I used those strong emotions to fuel the work I was about to do. Then I asked myself, silently and quickly, Is it me? My husband? The kids? The family?

My stomach tightened on the family. So I quickly rattled off each of my relatives' names.

In this case, I got a hit—a major, painful tightening of my solar plexus—on my great aunt and uncle. So I switched to my secondary follow-up questions and got a hit on Are they sick?

So then I asked myself silently, Is it serious? This time the response was a milder tugging at my solar plexus. Hmmm. I also felt frustration, but there was no real sense of urgency.

I let go of the energy and shook it off. I debated whether to take a shower and then call my great aunt and uncle or simply call them right then and there. But before I could decide either way, the phone rang. It was my great aunt calling to ask me to help her get my great uncle to the hospital. She is a strong woman, and having her ask for help surprised me.

I told her I would be over immediately, but she asked me to give her twenty minutes to get him packed and ready. My great uncle is a stubborn man, and my typically calm and serene great aunt sounded very frustrated with him. Seems their doctor wanted to admit him, and while this was not an emergency situation, the doctor wanted them to go straight to the emergency room, but my uncle flatly refused to go in an ambulance. I told her I would hit the shower, get changed, and be over in twenty minutes.

So by using the primary and secondary questions, I got it right on all counts: the relatives, there was an illness, it was serious but not urgent, but there was frustration. Using those questions to understand the premonition helped me to stay calmer because I'll admit that I was a little shaken that she had called to ask for my help.

When I arrived at their home, I was then able to assist in getting my great uncle loaded into their car—I kept him laughing and kept my great aunt from swatting him over the head with her purse. I followed them to the ER in my car and waited with them until he was admitted. A few days later, after a course of intravenous antibiotics, he was back home.

Despite what you may have heard or read, premonitions do not always spell disaster; they are often there to give you a psychic heads-up or an emotional lay of the land. All you have to do is learn to pay attention. You should use that emotional reaction that is swirling around you. It's going to be intense, so put it to work instead of letting it frighten you.

The next time you experience a premonition, try this technique: grab that energy, pull it in, and then use those preliminary questions followed by the secondary follow-up questions. It does not have to take more than a few seconds. Pay attention to how your body reacts to those questions.

Since premonitions are always emotional, expect a physical reaction. Watch for tugs at the heart center of the chest or your solar plexus region. You may simply experience a tightening in the chest or stomach or get that feeling of your stomach turning over. Focus on and follow the clues that your body gives you. This is both an easy and effective way to get to the bottom of premonitions.

Precognition

Precognition is our second type of psychic experience. It has many other names and titles; some of these you have probably heard of before. Precognition, or "precog" for short, is also called the sixth sense, the second sight, or the sight. People skilled in precognition are traditionally called seers.

> **Precognition:** The experience of having direct and detailed knowledge of the future by extrasensory means. The term precognition is also classically defined as the acquisition of paranormal (beyond normal) knowledge of the future.

For an easier way to remember what the word means, break it down: you have *pre,* meaning "before," and *cognito,* which means "to be known or no longer concealed."

With precognition, you don't have to ask yourself who, where, and what. A precognitive experience allows you to have clear and detailed information to work with and a means by which it is possible to predict the future. Precognition is experienced in many different ways. It can come in the form of psychic vision (clairvoyance), psychic hearing (clairaudience), psychic knowing or intuition (claircognizance), psychic empathy (clairsentience), or it can be kickstarted by psychic touch (clairtangency).

You may be wondering what triggers precognition; it's a good question. The answer depends upon the individual. However, we do know that precognition can be triggered by our relationships with or even proximity to other people. Also, precognition often comes roaring out to play during heightened emotional states.

You can expect stronger psychic experiences and more frequent occurrences when you are under stress or during a major transitional period of your life such as moving, starting a new job, getting married or divorced, kids graduating and heading off to college or grad school, and so forth.

Also being part of a large crowd can trigger precognitive experiences, especially if the crowd is wound up or excited.

Last but not least, let's not forget my personal favorite precognitive trigger: when the body's hormones are raging. Hormones play a big part in all psychic abilities, so you can expect that kids going through puberty and women during menstruation, pregnancy, and menopause tend to be psychic powerhouses. Oh—and no, I am not leaving the men out of this equation. For men, precognitive experiences will be stronger during those previously mentioned transitional periods of their lives. Also, men can expect that intense emotional times, be they happy or sad, will affect their psychic abilities as well. Honestly, gender plays no part when it comes to precognitive experiences.

Another way to experience precognition is through a precognitive dream. Most folks are going to have a mixture of precognitive experiences during their waking hours and some precognitive dreams. According to my research, about 50 percent of precognitive experiences occur during the dream state.

Which brings up the all-important question: How do you tell the difference between a regular dream and a precognitive one? Well, precognitive dreams always seem brighter, more vivid, louder, textured, and real. These types of dreams stand out. They typically startle you awake or you will remember the dream clearly upon rising.

In some cases, the precognitive information from the dream may not be remembered until the event plays out. When it does this at a later time, this causes the classic feeling of déjà vu. With déjà vu you have the sensation of repeating something that has already been experienced, seen, or felt. This memory from your own future, while familiar to you, still feels very strange. Then the déjà vu sensation jolts you into remembering your previous precognitive dream.

ONLY IN MY PRECOGNITIVE DREAMS

I should take a moment to point out that there are some individuals who only have psychic experiences through their dreams and not while they are awake. There is nothing wrong with that, nor should they feel slighted in any way. One of my close friends bemoans the fact that she does not have psychic experiences during her waking hours. She assumed this meant she had no psychic sensitivity at all. I explained to her that this was simply not the case.

There are a few reasons why this "precognitive dreams only" scenario can occur. First, the individual may be so busy or stressed during the day, their mind is so full that the only chance they have to unwind and allow their subconscious to come out and play is when they are asleep. So obviously they will receive their psychic information in their dreams.

Another circumstance is the person who secretly finds psychic experiences frightening. This unnerves them to the point that they close their minds down to the possibilities. However, if they are naturally strong psychics, then the only option is for the information to come forth during their dream state.

On the other hand, folks who only experience precognitive dreams may have had good reasons for shutting out the world on a psychic level. Perhaps they retreated into themselves as children to escape drama in the family dynamic or bitterly fighting parents. Refusing to acknowledge what was happening around them, they may have cut themselves off and hid, staying separate in a safe world where it was emotionally pain free, quiet, and calm. However, they may have done such a good job at this that now, as adults, they are blocked on a psychic level. It does happen.

Even an adult who has felt betrayed or hurt by others may choose to just "go into themselves" and block everything out for a time. If they purposefully shut themselves down and tune out everything else around them, and this practice becomes a habit, then the only way psychic information can be experienced for them is through their dreams.

Is it the end of the world if you only experience precognition through dreams? Of course not! If you only experience precognitive dreams, then break out the dream journal and date and document your dreams every morning when you wake up. Do this before you even get out of bed so you can record those images when they are fresh in your mind. Then later, when the precognition plays out, you can note the information and validate your experiences. Even if you only experience precognitive dreams occasionally, I would still log the information. In time, you will begin to see a pattern and understand what repeating themes or images mean to you.

The more you validate and accept your precognitive experiences, be they waking or asleep, the stronger they will become.

PRECOGNITION: A REAL-LIFE EXAMPLE
(OR, DON'T TAKE ME OUT TO THE BALLGAME)

To clarify our study of precognition, here is a story of a precognitive psychic experience. This one takes place at the ballpark, of all places. My son had scored great tickets from his work and had invited the family to go with him. I am not a baseball fan, but since one of my sons was out of town on a business trip and there was an extra ticket just sitting there, I said I would go along. It was a pretty spring day and a little chilly. However, we had prime seats just to the left of home plate and about twenty rows up from the field. While I find baseball boring, I was enjoying the game—sort of.

However, I lost count of the number of foul balls that went back up and over the fence at the game, at least six per inning. I asked my family if this was normal for a major league game and they said no, but to keep an eye out for a ball. Maybe we could get one.

Seriously? The last thing I wanted was a ball shooting my way at over ninety miles an hour. So I sat there trying to pay attention to the game, but my mind was starting to wander…because hey, it's baseball, and nobody is getting tackled like in football.

All of a sudden I *knew* a foul ball was going to come right at us and that it would not be pretty. I was sure of it. "Somebody's about to get really hurt by one of those foul balls," I said to my husband. Then I heard myself say, "They will be wearing a bright blue shirt and it will break their glasses."

My husband looked at me and said, "Honey, relax; it's a Cardinals game—everyone is wearing red."

"I'm serious. This is going to be nasty," I told him quietly, feeling sick to my stomach as I knew there was not a damn thing I could do about it. But after I had verbalized the precognition, I could see it clearly: bright blue shirt, broken glasses, blood. This was a precognitive experience. I just knew and spontaneously verbalized it, which allowed me to be able to see the scene play out in my mind.

Feeling a bit nervous, I silently and with a subtle gesture cast a quick protective circle around myself and my family to protect us from any foul balls. My husband caught the gesture, shook his head at me, and smiled. It wasn't hard to know what he was thinking—*Really? You're casting at the ballpark?* Ah well, he loves me anyway. Protection complete, I sat back in my seat and rubbed at a sudden sharp pain just above my left eyebrow.

The next batter came up and *bam!* He also hit a foul ball and it went up, up, and then over, and started to come down right in our section, just in front of where my family was sitting. Everyone in our section stood up, thinking they could snag the foul ball. I rose too; however, I looked up then, stayed perfectly still, and watched that damn ball come screaming down right in front of me.

As it landed, a man cried out in pain. Then the ball bounced hard off the poor fellow, I ducked, and it shot past the left side of my head. I ignored the mad scramble around me for the ball and focused on a man seated three rows in front of my family.

To my dismay, the older gentleman was grabbing his forehead and blood was rushing down the left side of his face. I heard someone yell for security, and then his wife asked people to look for his glasses. They found them two rows over in pieces. They had flown off when he was hit in the face by the foul ball.

My adult kids could not believe I let a foul ball go right past me, and I sat back down and watched as security escorted the man in the red jacket to the first aid station. Did my husband even react to my precognitive experience? Nope. He's used to me by now.

About a half-hour later, the older gentleman came back to a round of applause from our section. The team doctor had put a butterfly bandage on his temple to close the cut. He was in good spirits even though he had a hell of a bruise just above his left eyebrow. He announced to our section as he returned to his seat that the doctor had even bought him a beer.

It was then that I saw, now that his red Cardinal's baseball jacket was open, that the gentleman was wearing a bright blue polo shirt.

See the difference between premonition and precognition? With precognition I had specific information immediately. I knew an accident was about to happen, and then I heard myself describe what was about to happen. That spontaneous verbalization was not planned. I heard myself say it—it just popped right out of my mouth. And when I realized what I had said, that allowed me to get a better picture. Someone who was wearing a bright blue shirt would be hurt, and their glasses would be broken. Also interestingly, I then experienced a pain above my left eyebrow in the same vicinity as the gentleman who was struck by the ball.

There was no way in a crowded ballpark I could have warned everyone around me. But it did help me pay attention so I did not get hit by the ball's ricochet—otherwise there would have been two people with bloody faces and broken glasses.

Precognition can manifest in many ways; in this example, it came up as psychic knowing/intuition and as an empathic manifestation. Psychic knowing/intuition is technically called claircognizance. The best way to remember that is to know that this ability is what some describe as a sudden cognitive pop. I have personally always referred to this instantaneous awareness as the "psychic ping." In my mind it goes *ping!*—and then I either know, see, hear, or feel what is about to happen.

In this case, at the ballpark I also received a precognitive empathic manifestation as well, which would be correctly classified as clairsentience. I felt a sharp pain on my own face where the ball was about to strike someone else. At the time I did not realize that was what it was, as I was too busy watching that foul ball come down. But when the injured gentleman stood up to be escorted out to first aid, I realized with a start that he was cut right where I had felt that pain on my own forehead a few moments prior. Again, it was detailed information. See how this all connects? Precognition is a fascinating experience.

Postcognition

I find it interesting that whenever I bring up the term "postcognition" folks look at me and do a double take. Postcognition is more common than people realize, and it is a fascinating type of psychic experience.

> **Postcognition:** Sometimes called postcog or retrocognition,
> this is the experience of receiving extrasensory images or
> impressions from the past.

During a postcognitive experience, you gather or acquire by extrasensory means information about a person that they have already experienced or you obtain psychic information about an individual who has passed away.

Postcognitive episodes may be experienced through any type of psychic ability, as in psychic touch (clairtangency), psychic hearing (clairaudience), psychic knowing/intuition (claircognizance), psychic empathy (clairsentience), or a psychic vision (clairvoyance).

When it comes to clairvoyance, what is important to keep in mind is that a person who has clairvoyant abilities is technically having both precognitive and postcognitive experiences. (A true clairvoyant is classified as an individual who can see past, present, and future events.) However, postcognition may also be experienced through claircognizance (psychic knowledge/intuition) and also by being in a historic location such as a battlefield, for example, where you would experience through clairsentience (psychic empathy) the final emotions of the departed. And just to keep you on your toes, with a postcognitive clairaudient experience you would hear sounds such as voices, a battle, or even music from the past.

Postcognition can also occur though clairtangency (psychic touch). This particular psychic ability may occur by touching an antique object rich in history. The act of reading of an object's past is called psychometry. Through this, it is possible to gain psychic information from the past by holding a personal item or photograph of someone, be they living or deceased. The ability of clairtangency and the practice of psychometry will be covered in more detail in chapter 3.

The nifty part about postcognition is that you have the opportunity to check your facts and see if you are right because you are sensing what has already happened. Postcognition is also a handy skill for the paranormal investigator. Often there are cases where there is a residual haunting, which is simply considered to be old memories or a traumatic event that is playing back over and over again—the psychic energy from the event has seeped into the area and is on a loop. The residual haunting is probably one of the most common types of hauntings.

A postcognitive psychic will be the first to experience or pick up on this type of energetic information. Also, it is interesting to note that when psychically sensitive homeowners keep hearing music or voices in the home and there is no one there, this is a postcognitive experience and they are using the psychic ability of clairaudience. See how this all connects? It all starts with a psychic experience, and then that rolls into the ability.

Bottom line, all of us have psychic experiences, and these can come in very handy for all sorts of circumstances. The trick is to accept and learn from the psychic experience when it occurs. Now that you have some basic information on the three Ps of psychic experiences, let's move into our next chapter on psychic abilities and the four main ways in which they present themselves.

LOGIC TEACHES RULES *for*
presentation, not thinking.

Mason Cooley

Chapter 2

Psychic Abilities: Presentation, Identification, and Perception

Once you identify how your own unique abilities present themselves, then you can begin to work with these talents instead of feeling like you are simply along for the ride. So, without further ado, let's start by exploring how your psychic experiences manifest into your own specific varieties of natural psychic abilities.

To begin, the word *ability* is defined in several ways. Each of these possible definitions adds depth to the topic of personal psychic abilities:

> **Ability:** 1.) Power or capacity to do or act. 2.) Competence in an activity or occupation because of one's skill, training, or other qualifications. 3.) Talents, special skills, or aptitudes.

Did you notice that in the third definition we have the word *talent?* Talent is also synonymous with ability, aptitude, craft, capability, capacity, flair, skill, and savvy, just to name a few.

Do you see where I'm going with this? No matter what your knack or expertise, your own individual psychic abilities will present themselves in a way that will be unique to you. Psychic talents can also manifest in different combinations as well, again depending on the individual.

It is very important to stop and recognize just how you receive your own psychic information, as this identification will give you the clues you'll need to understand what psychic talents you are bringing to the table. Take a few moments and ask yourself in what ways your own psychic experiences present themselves.

Four Main Varieties of Extrasensory Perception: Identifying Your Own Innate Abilities

There are four main ways in which psychics perceive their extrasensory information: psychic knowing, hearing, seeing, and feeling. Now, just to be clear, this psychic knowing, hearing, seeing, and feeling are identified as being beyond the physical senses. These are the extrasensory perceptions.

In this identification process, personal observation is important—as you and only you will be able to recognize and then identify how your individual psychic abilities present themselves. Here is a brief rundown of the four main types of psychic abilities, which is followed by a more in-depth description of each of these individual talents. This way, you can discover more about yourself and which psychic path you are traveling down.

Oh, and before you wonder—yes, indeed, many people have more than one type of ability. You may, in fact, have *several* types of psychic abilities. We all have many talents and strengths. I would honestly be surprised if you didn't have a few different types of psychic abilities up your sleeve.

In order to help you pinpoint just what you are working with, see what you recognize about yourself. To begin, when you have had a precognitive experience, ask yourself exactly how you received the information. Remember, precognition is the experience of having direct and detailed knowledge of the future by extrasensory means.

- Did you "just know"? Did the information come quickly? Did the psychic information seem to spontaneously pop? That would be intuition, or psychic knowing, which is technically identified as **claircognizance**.

- Did you receive pictures or images? Did scenes play out in your mind's eye, giving you information about a past, present, or future event? That would be **clairvoyance**.

- Did your inner voice guide you? Did a song or phrase seem to have sudden meaning and then provide insight or did you hear what was meant but unspoken? Do you often "hear" another person's thoughts? This would be **clairaudience**.

- Did you have a physical sensation in your own body? Did you experience random emotions inconsistent with your own mood and then understand that you were picking up on someone else? This would be **clairsentience**, also known as psychic empathy.

Still not sure? Well, consider how you verbally describe your personal psychic experiences to another. Take a careful look at the language you are using. Seriously—sometimes we answer our own questions. We may just not always be paying attention to our own clues.

For example, if you tend to say I *just knew* or I *know (this) is going to happen*, then you are using claircognizance, or intuition. If you describe psychic experiences in terms of visual images and visions, that's clairvoyance. If you use phrases like *that sounds right* or *that sounds off*, and if you are listening in to what others cannot hear to receive your information, then yes, indeed, that is clairaudience. If you describe emotions and how they made you feel—*this room feels bad* or *that person made me feel uneasy* before anything else—then you are more clairsentient, or empathic.

Now that you have a general idea, let's get into the specifics of the main four types of psychic abilities. It is sometimes difficult to distinguish between different forms of ESP as they often meld and overlap with each other, and there are many opinions on the individual psychic talents that we can display. So I am making this as straightforward as possible, with some real-life examples of psychic abilities. I have always found that a real-life example helps others identify their own talents.

At the end of the day we should consider all types of psychic abilities, no matter how they present themselves in our lives. Each different variety of ESP is only one of many possible manifestations of the same psychic process. That's what makes it both challenging and thrilling all at the same time!

Claircognizance/Intuition: Psychic Knowing

A psychic intuitive is an individual who has an immediate insight or cognition. Claircognizance, or intuition, is one of the most common ESP abilities; it is also underestimated because it is so common. But I am here to tell you that intuition is powerful. It can be a tool and an ally. This ability is sometimes called "prophetic knowing" or the good old-fashioned gut hunch, that instantaneous awareness. It truly is an extrasensory knowing. Claircognizance literally means "clear knowing," and it is not a term we find readily when researching psychic abilities. However, it is the technical name for psychic intuition.

I consider psychic intuitives to be following the path of instinct. The area of the body where this claircognizant power is located is the solar plexus. The color associated with this ability is a bright, sunny golden-yellow. The gift of an intuitive is speed and spontaneity.

Now, to be clear, we should *not* confuse a gut hunch with a premonition. A gut hunch is a way to get your attention as the information rolls through. When a gut hunch occurs, the specific information is simultaneous. You feel it in the pit of your stomach. This information and the physical sensation in your belly occur at the same time. Thoughts and information seem to pop out of nowhere, and, in the simplest of terms, you just *know*.

With psychic intuitives there is an instant connection, and this sudden awareness or complete knowing happens very quickly. Claircognizance, or intuition, is a psychic ability that is amazingly fast, which allows an intuitive to go from insight to action right away. People who have strong intuitive abilities are typically spontaneous. They can shift gears and bounce from project to project, moving from topic to topic with dizzying speed and finesse. They are also terrific judges of character, and their first impressions of places and situations are very accurate.

Because this is a high-speed ability, psychic intuition, or claircognizance, is great for day-to-day problem solving. When it comes to intuition, you do not have to work out what a vision, another person's unspoken thoughts, or your emotions are telling you. Intuitives/claircognizants simply know, and that gives them a sense of guidance.

These folks tend to be in the right place at the right time because they just knew they had to be. Intuitives think fast on their feet and are great problem solvers, as they can adapt quickly to changing scenarios and situations. However, if an intuitive doesn't pay attention to those spontaneous pops of information, they can leave just as quickly as they arrived.

Also, intuitives can be endearingly frustrating to live with as they tend to just start talking about whatever is in their head at the moment, which can make the person on the other side of the conversation a little baffled as they try to figure out where that particular topic of discussion came from. Typically if the listener can wait a moment, they will discover that their intuitive friend was just several jumps ahead of them in the conversation. Look at it this way: if you know an intuitive, you will never be bored. Being a partner or friend with a claircognizant keeps you on your toes.

Pay Attention to It!

Here is a good example of intuition in the form of a misadventure while traveling. Several years ago (before everybody had GPS in their car and smartphones), I was invited to be the keynote speaker for a festival on the East Coast, and the night before the flight out I just knew something was going to go wrong. Even though I had a confirmed representative from the event picking me up from the airport, I could not shake the knowledge that I needed to print out driving directions to my hotel—something I have never done before or since.

Nevertheless, the night before my flight into Boston, I got on the Internet, found driving directions, and printed them out. My husband laughed at me for being so paranoid. After all, they had invited me and assured me that a driver who knew the area would be picking me up. Why was I so nervous about it?

I can honestly tell you that gut hunch combined with the overwhelming knowledge that I damn well better have directions on my person would simply not be ignored. So I tucked those printed directions in my purse and headed to the airport.

At the airport I stopped to grab a bottle of water and a seasonal Halloween magazine. I intended to pay for them with cash, but as I reached for the several singles I had in my wallet, the thought *save the cash* popped into my brain. My stomach tightened, and I knew that there would be a need for the singles within a few hours. I paid attention to the intuitive information and instead paid for my purchases with a debit card.

Later that afternoon I was picked up at the Boston airport by a mini-van crammed full of supplies for the outdoor festival, complete with two barking dogs and a very harried-looking couple. I cheerfully said hello, thanked them for picking me up, and climbed into the van. I ended up propping my suitcase on my lap, as there was no room for it anywhere else, and I prepared to make the hour and a half ride to the hotel, as the location of the event was about ninety miles away from the airport.

As we rolled out of the parking lot, the driver looked at me and announced, "I don't have any money. You'll have to pay the airport parking fee."

Now this was shocking to me, as my driver was actually the person in charge of the event. It was also rude, not to mention unprofessional, but I shut my mouth, dug out my cash, and asked the attendant for a receipt.

A few moments later, we came to the first of what would be many toll roads. The driver pulled up, stopped at the window, and looked at me expectantly. Since I did not want to find myself abandoned alongside the highway in rural Massachusetts, I said nothing and dug out the money for the toll. It was a good thing I had held onto all those singles!

As we made our way down the toll road and the dogs howled in the back seat, the driver looked at me and said in a very annoyed tone of voice, "So…I don't suppose that you know how to get to the hotel, do you?"

My heart gave a little jolt and I grabbed the printed directions out of my purse. "Actually, I *do* have driving directions. I had a hunch I would need these," I said.

The driver's mouth dropped open, and he made a comment about me living up to my reputation as a psychic. I had to navigate in a unfamiliar area, but at least I was able to get to the hotel.

As for how I got back to the airport after that event, a nice couple I had met at a different festival a year before offered to take me themselves.

Normally I would never even consider that. But when you are away from home and traveling on your own, you learn to take help when it is offered.

This friendly couple did have maps, and they made the trip back to the airport fun, even though at every toll road we came to it was a playful argument about who would pay the tolls. They made jokes the whole ride to the airport about how they had just known they would be getting to spend some real quality time alone with me…however, they had never imagined it would involve schlepping me around the state of Massachusetts to take me to the airport so I could catch a flight home.

Clairvoyance: Psychic Seeing

Clairvoyance is defined as the ability to perceive things that cannot be seen with the physical eye; instead, they are seen internally. Clairvoyants can see images and pictures that may be symbolic, or the experience can be as intense and detailed as watching a miniature psychic movie scene inside your mind.

A clairvoyant has powerful perception and insight into other people. Also as we mentioned earlier, clairvoyants are both postcognitive and precognitive. They can literally see the past (postcognition), the present, and the future (precognition).

I consider clairvoyants to be following the path of the visionary. Clairvoyance literally means "clear seeing." The third eye is considered to be the seat of clairvoyance. Located in the center of the forehead, this power center is the "screen" where those images and scenes play out. The color associated with this ability is a deep, vibrant indigo. The gift of a clairvoyant is art and color. They have an appreciation for and sensitivity to color that is intense.

How can you find your third eye for yourself? Well, close your eyes and then look inward and up. Take a deep breath in, then slowly let the breath out. Continue to take nice even breaths. Now deliberately shift your focus to the third eye area. What do you "see"?

Clairvoyants also find visual tools such as the tarot or runes to be stimulating. The images in the cards help to springboard them into a deeper, truer reading. (The topic of the tarot will be covered in more detail in chapter 5.)

Clairvoyance in Everyday Life

Clairvoyance can come in handy in your day-to-day life if you allow it—and that, my friend, is the real trick. Many folks are so uptight about their extrasensory perceptions that they never learn to enjoy them or roll with the advantages they can bring. Clairvoyants see past, present, and future. Often we are so caught up in the future that we overlook the fact that our psychic abilities were cluing us in on what is happening right now. No matter what your age—child, teen, or adult—the psychic ability of clairvoyance is easy and subtle to employ for present situations.

When I was young, one hot summer day my little brother went missing. My sister and I had checked with all of the neighbors on our street and searched in his usual hangouts, but he was nowhere to be found. He was simply gone. My mother was in a panic, and rightly so. She called the police, and my father rushed home from work. When I saw my parents standing on the front porch and crying in each other's arms, it really scared me.

I sat down in the front yard as we waited for the police and thought to my thirteen-year-old self: "If I were my brother, where would I go?" Suddenly a picture filled my head of my six-year-old brother alone in a new subdivision that was under construction. This new development was in an area adjacent to the subdivision we lived in. New roads had been paved, but only a couple of houses had started going up. Basically it was a kid's paradise of dirt hills and trails. Surely he wouldn't go there? He was not even allowed to go to the top of the street by himself.

In my mind's eye, I saw him climbing over a small dirt hill, laughing. As I watched the mini scene play out in my head, I saw a house on a corner that was getting a roof put on it. Without a word I stood up, jumped on my trusty ten-speed bike, and took off. My parents never even noticed.

I vividly remember how afraid I was. But the scene in my mind stayed true, and I knew that what I was seeing was happening right now. As quickly as I could, I rode out of our neighborhood and into the brand-new one where a couple of houses were just starting to be framed in.

As I rode into the new subdivision, I noticed there was a new house that I had never seen before being built on the corner. As I stopped my bike to catch my breath, I saw there were construction workers up on the roof nailing shingles into place. My heart thumped hard in my chest and I realized that this was exactly what I had been seeing in my mind. That meant I had to be close.

I crossed the street and slowly rode a little farther past the house, and then my six-year-old brother's blond head popped up from behind a large dirt hill. He climbed up to the top of the hill, dragging a piece of plywood, then jumped on it and slid down the hill fast. He landed with a thud and was laughing like a hyena. He was covered in dirt and having a blast.

I shouted his name, ditched my bike, and ran to him. I asked him how he had gotten so far from home by himself, and he simply stated that he wanted to see the new houses being built. Since I had a ten-speed and have never been particularly coordinated, I had to walk both my bike and my brother back home.

By the time we arrived home, the police were there. While my parents cried over my brother, I had to explain to a police officer how I had found him. I told the officer the truth. My parents said I was just lucky. The police officer said my brother was lucky to have a psychic for a sister.

I have actually used a similar technique when looking for lost items over the years. I stop, I sit down, and ask myself, "If I were _____ , then where would I be?" I take a deep breath, close my eyes, and hold very still. I turn my attention to the area of my third eye, and I wait and watch as a scene in real time plays out in my mind. Typically what I am shown is right on the money.

Clairvoyance is useful for everyday life: finding lost items and checking in remotely to see what your kids are up to or where your cranky boss is—or when your friend's kid decides to hide at the zoo. (Found him pretty quick too. Good thing, as his mother was not amused.) Clairvoyance in real time is great for locating wandering pets who decide to go cruise the neighborhood or even for finding younger siblings who go AWOL to sneak off and have an adventure.

Clairaudience/Telepathy: Psychic Hearing

A clairaudient, or telepath, receives extrasensory signals as a word, a sound, or even a song. Classically, telepathy is defined as the transmission of unspoken thoughts or psychic impressions from one person to another, while a clairaudient picks up words, sounds, music, or tones that are not discernible to the average ear. Simply put, a clairaudient "hears" their psychic information. Keep in mind that this psychic information is not heard in the physical realm; however, the information still has objective reality.

I consider clairaudients to be following the path of sound. The area of the body where this power is located is the region of the ears and throat. The color associated with this ability is a brilliant cobalt blue. The gifts of a clairaudient are listening and music. They hear the music of the mind, and they are able to perceive the tune of the universe.

Clairaudients can "hear" another person's private thoughts, and they may even receive impressions on another's mental state. Clairaudients can also hear what is meant but not spoken out loud—the best description of this would be "hearing between the lines." The clairaudient receives those psychic impressions in their mind's voice, not through their physical ears. This is paranormal hearing. Think of it as wearing psychic headphones.

So is there a difference between telepathy and clairaudience? Well, yes and no. Remember that telepathy is described as thought transference, which is the transmission of thought from one person to another independently of the recognized channels of the physical senses.

It is important to remember that clairaudience is often considered the one-sided reception of psychic information through sound. However, there are exceptions. Some clairaudients are both receivers and projectors. They can hear what someone thinks (or receive the message) and they can also project their thoughts for another person to hear internally. If they are both receiving and sending, then that means they are using telepathy.

Clairaudients can truly hear their own inner music. These individuals have keen sensitivity, and this makes them aware on a preternatural level. They also may be able to interpret another's hidden needs, as they can hear what someone else would never be able to verbalize on their own.

Sometimes clairaudients get grief or are teased for listening to the voices in their heads. What is important to realize is that the voice they hear is actually their own: it is their own inner monologue that is providing the information. So before you go and tease a clairaudient, keep in mind that there is no lying to one. After all, the word literally means "clear hearing." No matter what you say, they will hear the truth.

As a clairaudient, if other folks are in distress or thinking too loudly in your general vicinity, then you are going to pick up on that unfiltered information. So you will need to learn how to let it flow past you like background noise. In time, you will learn to distinguish the difference between what I like to call the psychic chatter of everyday stuff.

I find it helps to think of that psychic chatter like a radio playing softly in the background. You can listen to it but still go about your business. If the psychic information is important or dire, it tends to be louder and you will hear it clearly because the tone is different. It is that difference in psychic pitch that makes you tune in and focus on it.

An Example of Clairaudience and Clairsentience

A few years back I picked up a seasonal job as a floral designer. At the arts and crafts store I worked at, everyone was required to wear radio headsets so, like it or not, you heard a constant stream of conversations.

Typically I turned mine down as low as possible and tended to ignore them, but to my surprise and the vexation of my coworkers, it did allow me to brush up on my clairaudience. I will admit that it was almost comical how many times I turned in my headset or got a different one, thinking there was something wrong with it. It took me a couple of weeks to realize what I was actually hearing.

Once it dawned on me, I was excited by the unexpected perk. So I turned an annoyance into a tool and learned how to let that background noise flow right past me. It wasn't long at all before I was able to differentiate between background conversations and psychic information.

The first thing I detected with having that constant stream of talk in my ear was that any clairaudience I experienced was louder in my mind than the background noise. It had a sharper, clearer tone. Also, I began to notice that my psychic hearing would kick in with a vengeance if the person whose thoughts I was "overhearing" was in my general area. Since I worked in a high-stress store with many unhappy employees, it made for very loud psychic listening. It's a general rule of thumb that the angrier or more upset someone is, whether they realize it or not, the louder they can project their thoughts.

One day during Thanksgiving weekend I was in the store before it opened, cranking out seasonal floral arrangements as fast as I could. Since we were not open for business, the majority of other employees were stocking shelves, which made me feel like I had the place all to myself. To add to the drama, the district manager was on hand, terrorizing his underlings and prepping for the big weekend-long sales.

Being typically antiestablishment, I was not wearing my earpiece; instead, I had it draped around my neck. The district manager had reminded me to put on my headset when he had walked by me earlier, and my straight-faced reply was "I tremble and obey."

He barked with laughter, my manager sent me a death glare, and I left the earpiece untouched and still dangling around my neck.

Anyway, as I was working up holiday centerpieces, I kept hearing the same words all rushed together: "Oh my god please don't let me pass out, please don't let me pass out…"

This was a very different tone than my normal hearing, and it was underneath the holiday music that was blasting through the in-store stereo system. Deliberately, I stopped what I was doing and looked around. I held still and listened hard with my physical ears.

Nope, there weren't any employees around my workstation. Shrugging it off, I went back to work for a few minutes until I started to hear the phrase again.

This time I closed my eyes and concentrated. I kept hearing that voice—it seemed softer, almost weaker now, but more urgent, as if the person was in more emotional distress. How did I know? Well, my heart started to race, and I felt lightheaded myself. I took a cleansing breath and connected to the earth by planting my feet and visualizing myself as a tree sinking roots into the ground.

After a couple of seconds I felt better. However, I now knew that I was picking up on someone else in that store, and I was using both clairaudience and clairsentience (psychic hearing and psychic empathy). To double check that I was not just overhearing someone on the headset, I tucked the earpiece into place and turned up the volume. Other than the occasional back and forth between the unseen folks stocking the shelves, there was nobody asking for help—not out loud, anyway.

Then in my mind I heard a soft crying. I felt an overwhelming panic and fatigue, and I almost started to cry myself. That was it. I had to find out what was going on.

I tossed my wire cutters on the counter and went looking. I let the voice I was psychically hearing, combined with the emotions I was sensing, lead me to where I needed to go. Remember that game you played as a kid where you had to find something, and if you were far away they would announce you were cold, if you were moving closer they would say you were getting warmer, and when you were closer still they would say you were hot? And if you were right on top of it, they would announce something like, "You are so hot, you should be burning up!"

Well, this was very much like that child's game. I knew I was getting warmer by how much more intensely I could feel the emotions and hear that voice. I honed in on it and let it draw me to where I needed to go. I briskly marched several aisles down, turned a corner, and found the source of the distress almost hidden behind a big rolling rack filled with boxes of product.

It was one of the college-age employees. As I walked closer to her, I could actually hear her whispering to herself, "Oh my god, please don't let me pass out…"

I called her name sharply and as she looked up at me, I saw that her face was horribly swollen. As I reached out, her typically gorgeous complexion turned an interesting shade of pale green. She staggered and started to fall. I pounced on her, lowered her to a sitting position on the floor, and then put her head between her knees.

Being a mom, I took one look at those swollen cheeks and realized that she had must have just had her wisdom teeth out. As she spoke to me, I could see that she still had those gauze pads in her mouth to slow the bleeding of her gums! I also knew (after going through this with all three of my own kids) that you are not supposed to do any heavy lifting right after the surgery.

The poor thing was so afraid that she would get fired because she had to have her wisdom teeth removed over Thanksgiving break that there she was at work less than twenty-four hours after oral surgery—on her feet and lifting heavy boxes over her head, no less. I picked her straight up off the floor—she was a tiny thing—and called to the manager on duty over my headset.

Then I basically carried the girl to the back room. The whole way back there she cried and worried she would be fired if she went home. I told her kindly to shut up and trust me. I used my "mom voice"—in other words, I pushed confidence and trust at her with the sound of my voice.

Technically that was a form of telepathy wherein I sent and she received. It worked like a charm.

As I hauled her into the back room, where the district manager was speaking on the phone, I announced that we had a coworker who had fainted and needed to go home. That district manager took one look at us, gasped, and rushed to grab the young woman a chair.

Fifteen minutes later, with the district manager's blessing, I personally escorted the young lady into her friend's car with the promise that she would stay off her feet for the rest of the weekend. Her friend told me she would sit on her if necessary and that she would also take her back to the oral surgeon that very afternoon. A week later, the young woman was back at work, her swelling was completely gone, and she was doing great. She was a little spooked by how I had found her, but she took it in stride.

This was an interesting lesson to learn. While I had never considered myself particularly adept at clairaudience, wearing a headset at that seasonal job did allow me to brush up on my psychic hearing. You could easily try something like this at home. Just wear your earbuds from your iPod or smartphone and put the music on low—loud enough that you can hear it but soft enough that it becomes background noise and you can still hear conversations around you. Using this tip, see what you can discover about your own clairaudient talents.

Clairsentience/Empathy: Psychic Feeling

A clairsentient is commonly known as an empath. Empaths have the ability to sense emotional energy both from the people around them and the environment they happen to be in. A clairsentient is a person who can physically tune in to the emotional experiences of another person or place. They sense attitudes, emotions, and sometimes physical ailments.

I consider clairsentients/empaths to be following the path of emotion and the heart. The area of the body where their power is located is, of course, the heart. There are two colors associated with this ability: glowing emerald green and a vibrant rosy-pink color. The empaths' gift is their awareness of others and the depth of their compassion.

Clairsentience is a complex concept and one that is often misunderstood or confused with clairscence (which translates to "clear smelling") or clairtangency (which means "clear touching"). Clairsentience literally means "clear feeling," and I think this is why folks continue to use the terms *empath* to identify a person with this ability and *psychic empathy* as the ability itself.

Remember that a clairsentient, or empath, is a person who acquires psychic knowledge primarily by means of empathic feelings and emotions. This also means they have the psychic ability to project their senses out a short distance away from their own body and sense the environment around them. So if you often describe how an environment or person close to you makes you feel, and you trust that impression before anything else, take a wild guess at what you are actually doing. You are, in fact, projecting with your clairsentience, gathering psychic information, and reading the emotions and energy around you!

The ability to sense or experience the feelings and emotions of other people is a double-edged sword. People may be drawn to clairsentients/empaths as they are often so caring and kind that they sometimes (without meaning to) absorb other people's problems. So clairsentients/empaths have to be alert and not take on extra drama in their life.

When psychic empathy is not acknowledged, clairsentients/empaths have no idea where those extra, unwanted emotions are coming from or why their mood can suddenly take a dramatic turn for no apparent reason. It can also explain why many empaths avoid hospitals and intensely dislike doctor's offices or crowded, noisy places. For clairsentients/empaths, it is automatic psychic overload to be around many people who are ill or in pain. Furthermore, the rush and psychic energy of a large crowd of people can feel overwhelming and emotionally toxic.

How do you avoid this problem? Well, for starters, being aware is half the battle. If you need to be in a large crowd, then make sure that you take the time afterwards to recharge quietly and have some peace and quiet. A little solitude will do you a world of good. If this topic of psychic recovery intrigues you, rest assured that we will cover psychic first aid in detail in chapter 8.

Clairsentients/empaths have the innate ability to sense emotional and energetic vibrations simply by being near a highly charged environment. They can directly and consciously be in tune with another person's emotional state by choice or by accident. For many clairsentients/empaths, the psychic information manifests as a physical reaction or sensation—as in the story I just shared about the college girl at work who was ill. I felt her emotional distress and her lightheadedness like they were my own physical symptoms.

This particular type of extrasensory perception allows clairsentients/empaths to experience what those around them are emoting or are just about to express. Empaths are literally going to feel the information: it may come as a tingling or a rush of fear or as emotions such as an overwhelming joy or sadness.

Clairsentient ability can also manifest as a mirror of the pain from the person they are picking up on. Recall the story from the last chapter about the gentleman who got hit by the foul ball. I felt a sharp pain on my own forehead in the area where he was struck a few moments before it actually happened. Psychic empathy is a complex ability—one that can present itself in myriad ways. Take the time to investigate this talent for yourself and see what you discover about your own psychic abilities.

No matter if you are claircognizant, clairvoyant, clairaudient, or clairsentient, it is worth your time to focus on your own abilities. Keep notes of your psychic experiences. Write down how these manifested and, most importantly, which psychic ability or abilities you seem to be working with the most often. I urge you to pick up a journal or spiral notebook and turn that into a psychic journal. The best person to tell you what talents you are bringing to the table is yourself.

Now join your hands, and
with your hands your hearts.

Shakespeare

Chapter 3
Clairtangency and Psychometry

The ability of clairtangency is not typically mentioned with the most recognized of the "big four" classic psychic abilities: claircognizance/ intuition, clairvoyance, clairaudience, and clairsentience/empathy. Clairtangency is misinterpreted or mislabeled to the point that researching it is often a very frustrating exercise. In order to avoid that, I decided to devote an entire chapter to this particular psychic ability. Also, it is not unusual to find the topic of clairtangency lumped together or confused with clairsentience/empathy, but they are two different things altogether.

This mix-up happens easily enough, as clairsentience means "clear feeling," so folks mistakenly assume that this means "clear feeling" as in touch, when actually it is "clear feeling" as in *emotion*. In order to be crystal clear, let's go over the definitions of both of these different psychic abilities one more time:

> **Clairsentience:** Also called psychic empathy, clairsentience is defined as "clear feeling." Clairsentients, or empaths, can sense and obtain psychic information through the energies and feelings of others as well as the emotions that are around them or in their general vicinity.

> **Clairtangency:** Clairtangency is defined as "clear touching." With clairtangency—more commonly known as psychometry—psychic information is gathered by the corporeal, or physical, touch of the hands. For example, if you touch someone, as in a handshake, and receive psychic information, this is an act of psychometry and you are employing the psychic ability of clairtangency.

I think where the waters become muddied is that folks tend to assume that the reading of an object is psychometry, while the reading of a person is clairtangency. That's like saying six to one and half dozen to the other. Once again: clairtangency is the psychic ability, while psychometry is the act itself of reading an object or a person.

Clairtangency and Postcognition

Clairtangency can be experienced as either a precognitive or postcognitive event. However, it has been my experience that the ability of clairtangency and the act of psychometry have stronger links to postcognition, or the psychic sensing of the past. You may be wondering what good postcognition would be during a reading. Well, you'd be surprised. It comes in very handy during a psychic reading. For example, I typically pick up postcognitive information about the people or objects that I touch with deliberate psychic intention. When I experience glimpses of their past, I am basically sensing and/or receiving a flash of insight about the person they are and what major life experiences they have had. This helps me to connect to them and give a better psychic reading.

When it comes to the deliberate touching of an object with psychic intention, the process is very similar to reading the psychic energy of a person. This is because all objects have their own unique energy fields, and these energy fields have absorbed vibrations from the people and places around them. When performing a psychometry reading of an object, classically you are holding the object in your receptive hand, using the ability of clairtangency ("clear touching") and then connecting with the energy patterns that were left behind on the object from its former and current owners. Bottom line: as you are psychically reading the past that surrounded the object, you will be having a postcognitive experience.

Items such as rings, jewelry, keys, clothes made from natural fibers, and other similar possessions such as wallets or a uniform hat are typically used in a psychometry reading, as they are the most personal. When an object has been constantly worn (jewelry) or habitually carried on the person (a wallet or a set of keys), then the objects themselves retain some of the owner's energy. Metal objects such as jewelry and keys tend to hold onto psychic impressions for longer periods of time. Metal is simply a good conductor for electricity and psychic energy. It is commonly thought that the human aura leaves an electromagnetic imprint on everything that it touches, so just imagine what can happen when a human is in contact with a metal object for years at a time.

The longer the item is owned, worn, or used, the deeper and clearer the energetic imprint becomes on the item. This is where a postcognitive experience comes in, since when you read an object during the act of psychometry, you are actually reading the item's history.

The Art of Psychometry

There are three types of psychometry readings: objects/photographs, locations, and people. We will start with objects/photographs as this is the most common, and it is classic. The process itself is pretty simple. With the ability of clairtangency, you can read an object by touching it, holding it in the palm of your receptive hand (which is the opposite of the one you write with), or holding the item up against your own body. If the item being read is small, such as a ring, hold it in your own hand and then press your hand against one of the points on your own body that corresponds to your most prevalent psychic ability.

Think about it: if your abilities lean toward clairvoyance and you "see," then the forehead, or third eye area, is the way to go. If you tend to be more intuitive, then go for the solar plexus. Perhaps you are clairaudient and "hear" your psychic information? Then holding the small item at the side of your face, just next to your physical ear, would be best. Lastly, should you have stronger empathic abilities, then I would hold the object close to your heart.

To be clear, the seat of power for a clairvoyant is the third eye (forehead) area. The solar plexus is the power spot for an claircognizant/intuitive. The ear/side of the face area is the best place to amplify your impressions as a clairaudient. Finally, as empaths/clairsentients, the power source would be the place where all of your own emotions spring from: the heart. These are the four points on the body where there are the most active receptors for psychic impressions through psychometry. This is a nifty little trick that increases your ability to give an accurate and more in-depth psychometry reading, and it uses the ability of clairtangency in combination with your other most prevalent psychic ability.

Now let's take a look at those three main types of psychometry readings.

Reading Objects and Photographs

What can an object tell you? Oh, I thought you'd never ask. All inanimate objects have their own unique energy impressions. These impressions, or vibrations, are gathered from the people and places the object is associated with.

How much you can actually tell about the past owners will depend on the object's history. For example, if a ring was handed down from mother to son, and then the son gave the ring to his wife, and then someday she passed it on to her daughter...well, then, you might pick up many different postcognitive impressions. There would be the memories and impressions from the original owner, her son and daughter-in-law, and then the current owner, the granddaughter, especially if the granddaughter has or had very strong emotional ties to her grandmother, the original owner of the ring. There is power in loving emotions, and if this is the case, you could get a very strong psychic impression of the ring's original owner. Honestly, it won't matter if the original owner is living or deceased; if there is love, there is a link. If there is a link, then you can follow that and uncover that postcognitive psychic information. This is especially important to keep in mind when it comes to reading photographs.

In the simplest of terms, a photograph is a reproduction of the person you are reading. Yes, that little piece of paper, color, and chemicals is now a miniature doorway of sorts. I like the term *doorway* because it gives you an "in" straight into that individual the reading is focused on. All you have to do is take a deep breath and step right in. It is important to allow yourself to experience this. Do not think the process to death. Really look at the person in the photograph, see them, then ask yourself what your first impressions are.

I find doing psychometry readings with a photograph to be a big help. It is important to comprehend that while you are looking at the image of the person in the photograph, you are already one step closer to connecting than you were with an object like keys or jewelry. When that person's picture was taken, their energy was present. Oh, and before someone panics: the energy is represented, or symbolized, if you will; it is not captured in or by a photograph. It is that *symbolic* energy that you are sensing/reading by holding the photo in your hands.

Also, it won't matter if the person in the photograph is living or deceased. There are no boundaries to that represented energy or the person's energetic essence, if you like, symbolized in the photograph. Holding the photograph allows you to connect, step into the picture, and see, hear, know, or feel.

Here is a little tip to consider: when it comes to reading someone else's cherished photos, I do *not* recommend that you hold the photograph to one of those previously mentioned four main psychic areas (forehead, side of the face, solar plexus, or heart). People are protective of older and fragile photos, plus doing that with a photograph tends to freak people out. I would leave the photo on the table and just allow your fingertips to touch the edges or you can just hold it in your hand. Now relax your face and body, then look at and into the photograph.

I do want to caution you against trying to perform a psychometry reading by looking at a photo from a smartphone. Let the client hold up the phone for you to see, but you should keep your clairtangent hands off it. Why, you may wonder? Well, think about it: What would you actually be reading if you held the client's phone? They have that phone on themselves constantly, and the phone does have metal parts... Come on, you've figured this out by now. If you hold the cell phone to look at a picture, then you will probably end up reading the phone itself and the phone's owner, not the image on the device.

Also, electronics and psychic ability notoriously do not mix well. You could accidentally screw up their phone and they would have to reset it or, worse, buy a new one. Surely you will have noticed by now that when your own psychic abilities are on full blast, your electronic equipment, phones, and computers tend to act up. We will be discussing the phenomena of electronic snafus and psi abilities in detail in chapter 6.

Reading Locations

When you get right down to it, using the ability of clairtangency to read a location is only slightly different than reading an object or a photograph. The difference is that you won't be holding an object or photograph in your hands; instead, you will be placing your hands on the ground, furniture, floor, or even the walls. You can also stand quietly with your palms turned out and your arms and hands resting comfortably at your side. Then allow the energies to come to you and into your open palms.

Many times, people who are unaware that they are clairtangent enter an environment such as an old graveyard, historic home, or battlefield and unexpectedly gather psychic impressions by running their hands over objects. I often hear people rhapsodize about their amazing empathic abilities, but—one more time—if you are touching things and getting specific information about the past, then you are having a postcognitive experience and you are using the psychic ability of clairtangency, not empathy.

Technically, reading a location using clairtangency means you are going to have to touch things in one form or another, and this in and of itself can be quite the challenge, if not outright forbidden. My daughter is currently getting her master's degree in museum sciences, so I hear her complaining a lot about why some historical sites should be protected to prevent further damage by the public, and that artifacts should not be touched unless the curators are wearing gloves. The few times we have gone to a museum together recently, she gave me an (unnecessary) lecture because she knows I am itching to touch the artifacts so I can really read them. (In case you are wondering, I never have. Not on purpose anyway.)

When my children were small, I once accidentally brushed my elbow against a sarcophagus that was out in an open room at the art museum. I was scooping up one of my toddlers who was having a meltdown at the time. That accidental brush almost knocked me on my ass. It made an impression: it was like a brush with thunder. However, I was horrified and still break a sweat at knowing I brushed an artifact. Since my daughter remembers that story now, twentysomething years later, she frowns and lectures. It's sort of endearing. I would never dream of touching an artifact without permission, but I will admit that it's a little fun to yank her chain.

Also, anyone who has ever toured a historic location or home knows that touching museum-quality pieces or even the walls of a historic home with your hands is typically not an option. So how *do* you get a feel for the location?

The easiest way around this is to allow your whole body to be the receptor. Your feet are standing on the floor of the house or the land, the very earth of the location, aren't they? Well, there you go. The location in New Hampshire called America's Stonehenge revealed many secrets to me. My friend Christopher took me there recently, and it was incredible. All I had to do was stand there and pull the energy up through the soles of my feet while I stood in the walking areas of the site. I closed my eyes, felt the breeze coming through the trees in the park, and opened my hands to allow the location's energies and its past information to come to me.

There was one chamber we were allowed to go into. I crouched down with my hands palms-up on my knees, and then I stayed put a few moments to see what I could sense using clairtangency. I visualized the information coming to me through my feet and the open palms of my hands. Whoa baby, what a rush!

By using clairtangency this way—pulling the energies into your palms or, in a pinch, through your feet via the ground you are standing on—it is possible to safely obtain psychic impressions of the important events and the people who lived, worshipped, and died in an area, all while leaving historic locations and artifacts untouched and preserved for everyone else to enjoy.

Reading People

Last but not least, we come to reading people. There are many books on the market that can teach you the physical clues to watch for in "people reading." However, that is not what I am speaking of here. There is more to clairtangency than being a sensitive person who is able to feel sympathetic for their client or be a better-than-average body language reader. Using clairtangency to read an individual by touch goes a lot further. When you are reading another person using clairtangency, you are interpreting the energy that is being transmitted directly to you from their hand and into yours; then you verbalize your impressions for the client.

This is easy enough to do, but there are a few steps in the process. First off, always, *always* ask permission to touch when you are performing a reading using clairtangency. I smile directly at the client and say, "Do you mind if I hold your hand and look right into your eyes? It will help me to get better information."

I find it safer to announce my intentions beforehand because direct, prolonged eye contact with a stranger, not to mention handholding, can give people the wrong impression. The majority of the time, and if I have never read for them before, the clients say sure and then casually reach out for my hands.

I always hold my hands back and caution them with, "I am asking permission because once I touch you, I'm in." Then I smile again to soften the warning. That might make them blink at me a couple of times and reconsider.

Now, am I telling you this because I am so freaking amazing? Ah, no. I'm telling you this because I am honest. And if you are talented at clairtangency, then honest is something you are going to have to be with the people whom you read from now on.

When clairtangency is purposely involved, you are much better off announcing what you are doing and why *before* you touch anyone. Bottom line: you are going to have them at an unfair advantage. Clairtangency is strong, and it kicks open the door so that all of the other psychic abilities you have can come out and play. There is no such thing as "Oh, I can do psychometry *sometimes*." Let's be honest here. Yes, I use that word a lot, don't I? Honesty goes hand in hand with ethics and honor.

Now, I will admit that 90 percent of the time people just shrug and smile at me because they really don't believe me about the clairtangency. That tends to change after about five seconds or so, once I have ahold of them and I link in. The reactions vary according to the individual. Some folks jolt in their chair, some smile, some go very quiet, and some get teary eyed; their breath catches, and then they all get very still.

Once I have their attention, I blow past any of the tension that I feel from linking in with a stranger by taking a nice even, deep breath. Then I tell them what I see, hear, know, and feel. I am a mixed bag of psychic abilities, but I have come to realize that clairtangency is probably one of my strongest psychic abilities, and everything else often seems to flow from that.

What does it feel like to link in using clairtangency? It is like being hyperaware in a very quiet way. It is not a trance—my eyes do not roll back in my head, nor do I sway in my chair for dramatic effect. As for myself, I am always very aware of everything going on around me while I am performing a reading.

But the way to describe how it feels when I have made a connection is like an inner click—then I know that I'm linked in. I have been told that my eyes shift back and forth and it looks as if I am "reading" very fast when I gaze into the client's eyes. My hands get warmer and, once I feel and hear that inner click, it all smooths out and I float along, allowing the impressions to come to me.

I only hold onto the client's hand for a few minutes; that is plenty of time. Also, I should point out that I do not grab or take information, which would be unethical and, quite frankly, unfair. I let the impressions and psychic information flow, wash over, and come to me in their own way. I verbalize what I see, hear, or feel to the client as I continue with the reading.

I know it's time to let go when I feel a strain in my hands and my solar plexus starts to ache. So I give their hands a friendly little squeeze before I let go and sit back. Removing my hands by putting them in my own lap and off the table breaks the link and helps to clue in the client that that particular part of the reading is over.

Clairtangency and Blocking Unwanted Personal Information

I first discovered many years ago when I worked the local psychic fairs that if I held a person's hand and looked them square in the eyes, I was "in." It gave me an unexpected edge and was my fallback if I had a difficult reading. I knew, saw, and felt important events about the client and their past. Occasionally I would hear names in my mind or, like that old charades game, it was a name that sounded like something else and I had to work out what I was hearing—you know, *second syllable, sounds like?* This gave me names, feelings, faces, and events. I still use this technique today if I am having a difficult reading or a client prefers that I not use tarot cards.

Eventually I learned that this meant I had the ability of clairtangency. Back in the day, when I first opened the door on this ability, I will admit that it gave me a hell of a fight whenever I wanted to get it closed again. For a while, each and every time I shook someone's hand, I would get unwanted personal information—so I was hoisted by my own petard. That sent me scrambling for answers, and eventually I learned to block the clairtangency.

How? Well, I experimented. Through trial and error, I quickly figured out that if I am in a social situation and cannot avoid the handshake or the casual hug, then I take a deep breath and in my mind (not out loud) think *block!* Then I energetically push back against the other person's information and let go of the other person's hand or get out of the hug as quickly as possible.

The time I see a problematic scenario coming and know that I can't dodge the individual, I now know what I need to do. I think almost all of us know people like that: that annoying person who hugs too long or never lets go of your hand, or the classic emotional vampire who always wants to be held and petted and adored. So I mentally "set" myself, sort of like I do before I lift heavy weights or I imagine a martial artist would do before executing a kick.

Once I am "set," then I visualize the annoying person's aura. I see it reaching out, and then I picture mine pushing theirs back politely but firmly. I send a small energetic push at them. It's not a slap; it's a firm bump. I raise up the energy from my solar plexus and visualize that it pushes back at the other person's unwanted psychic information.

Sometimes if the annoying party is sensitive, they may notice the push; if they do, it only makes them let go of me faster. The range of reactions varies from startled to horrified to confused to (my personal favorite) fake hurt feelings from an emotional vampire (wherein the emo-vamp knew they were being emotionally pushy and you just shut them down). And you know what? I can live with that. Just because you have the ability of clairtangency does not mean you have to be forced to endure everyone else's personal information or inappropriate psychic leeching.

The "set and push back" and "block" tricks work fairly well for me the majority of the time, and if for some reason they don't, then I just allow any unwanted psychic information to wash over and past me. This tends to leave a bit of residue or vague impressions behind, but I stoically ignore it. Typically someone has to be pretty pushy or obnoxious for me not to be able to block them out.

Honestly, when it comes to a quick, impersonal, or professional "hello" type of handshake or even the casual one-armed hug, you can easily block any psychic impressions. It's only the obnoxious, emotionally manipulative individuals—who try to hang on for a longer amount of time than would be considered socially acceptable—who cause problems for most psychics. Use those "block" and "set and push back" techniques. You can use this practice and not be nasty about it on an energetic level. Just be polite and firm. It works like a charm.

Clairtangency Practice, Anyone? (It's Easier Than You Think!)

Recently I was a featured speaker at a large event, and one of the topics I lectured on was psychic abilities and how to figure out what variety you possess. While I was explaining clairtangency, I looked out into the crowd of a couple hundred people and sized them up. They understood the concept but did not understand how they could use this to pinpoint their own psychic abilities, so I announced that I was going to give them a chance to see for themselves just how clairtangency worked and rolled into other psychic abilities. I pulled off one of my rings and scanned the crowd.

There was a nice, friendly faced guy sitting near the aisle who had been listening very attentively to the lecture. I walked up to him and asked him which hand he wrote with. He was a lefty, so I asked him to hold out his right hand. I explained that the hand you write with is considered to be a dominant and projective hand, while the other was considered to be a receptive hand—all the better with which to receive psychic impressions.

I told him that I wanted him to close his receptive hand around the ring and then tell me what popped into his mind. What did he see, know, hear, or feel? The room was hushed, and the guy balked. He was clearly very nervous. I smiled at him and told him to relax and not think about it. He got more tense. Then I playfully snapped my fingers in front of his face, and he jolted. I bent over, smiled in his face, and told him, "Relax—I haven't bitten anyone all day." That made him laugh, and then his eyes got very large.

Looking surprised, he said, "Husband, gift, love, memory."

I smiled at him and asked him if he knew, heard, felt, or saw those words. He remarked that he knew—that they had just popped into his mind. I followed up by asking if there was any emotion attached to the information. He replied there was not. He looked stunned by what he had just done, and I asked him to sit tight.

Then I randomly chose a woman a few rows over and asked for her receptive hand. Her remarks were "blue, ocean, romance, love." She said that she saw and felt those words.

I handed the ring to a third person, who came up with "anniversary and surprise." He announced that he had seen a misty picture or scene play out in his head.

I took the ring back and told the crowd that the pearl ring was a gift from my husband to me on our thirtieth wedding anniversary. He had surprised me by giving it to me while we were on the beach in Florida. That trip was one of our favorite memories.

The folks in the crowd were astounded to discover just how accurate those three people had been, each in their own way. I used this as an opportunity to show how the three people's remarks had indicated where their strongest psychic abilities rested.

Take a look at the comments from the first gentleman. He stated that he "just knew," with no emotional ties, and that the words had popped into his head. That's claircognizance/intuition, and very accurate too, I might add. The second person used words that were visual and emotional in nature. She also said that she saw and felt those words, meaning that she was using both clairvoyance and clairsentience/psychic empathy. Finally, our last volunteer really honed in with two words, remarking that he had seen a picture in his mind of a scene, meaning he had used clairvoyance. He even followed up with another comment afterwards while I explained the results to the crowd. He asked if I had been wearing a green dress when I was given the ring. I had been wearing a swim suit and we were sitting on the beach, watching the ocean.

After I got home from the event, I checked the scrapbook I had made from our anniversary trip and got a jolt when I realized that the beach chairs we were sitting on when my husband gave me that ring were, in fact, dark green. Wow! *There* was the green he had seen. I mentioned before that clairvoyants tend to be drawn to colors—here was a perfect example.

Putting those three people on the spot was a good way to keep them from not thinking the process to death. They just said the first things that came to mind, and each of them was correct. It was fun to watch them discover something new about themselves. Try it out for yourself. Have fun and relax; it truly does work better that way. Clairtangency is a fascinating psychic ability and well worth the time to develop and practice.

IF YOU WERE born to be a medium,
you will not wonder if you are;
you will know it.

John Edward, *Infinite Quest*

Chapter 4

Mediumship

Mediumship is a wildly popular topic these days. Thanks to reality TV, lots of folks like to tack the term *medium* on their list of psychic accomplishments. However, mediumship is not a skill you just pick up. You can't study a couple of books and become a medium overnight. You cannot copy the terms and style of a television psychic and turn into a medium either. It simply does not work that way.

So why am I writing about the topic, then? Because I think it's way past time to put some straight-up, honest, and useful information out there about mediumship. So brace yourself; if you want to understand mediumship, then be prepared to deal with the realities. I am about to make a very bold statement that may either annoy or thrill many people. Here it is—are you ready? *When it comes to being a medium, you either are one or you are not.*

If you have the innate ability, you will be able to employ it. This is not an easy or comfortable psychic ability to wield. It's emotional, raw, and sometimes overwhelming.

For many years, I thought the information I was receiving during a reading when I used my clairtangency was strictly postcognitive information, as I was seeing, knowing, and feeling the client's memories, and sometimes even hearing the names of their loved ones. I figured that was all it was—just postcognitive information. When clients started calling me a medium, I secretly found that hilarious. You have to understand, in the early 1990s, psychic fairs were colorful events with lots of interesting characters. Some readers actually wore turbans! And there I sat, a young woman in her late twenties looking as normal as the day was long. Then a funny thing happened while I was so busy chuckling about being a postcognitive psychic who was accidentally being called a medium. The ability began to develop. No turban required. Stubbornly, I refused to admit to myself what was happening. It was postcognition, I told myself, and nothing more.

Many years passed. I was in full-time author mode and occasionally when I would do an author event I would get requests to do clairvoyant readings. If my schedule allowed it, I would because I figured it was a good way to keep those psychic abilities in shape and on track. About eight years ago, I was holding a client's hand for a reading and she demanded—not asked, *demanded*—that I try to contact her mother who had passed on.

I was a little startled by the ultimatum. I remember asking her what made her think I could just "contact" her mother for her. Her response was that she had heard from her friends that I was a Witch; after all, who better than a Witch to contact the dead? I remember starting to giggle helplessly because not only is that incorrect, but it struck me as a very hilarious and Hollywood-type of assumption. Jeez.

The client raised her voice at me and made her demand again. Then she made a fateful move. She leaned into my personal space, squeezed my hand too hard, and yanked me forward across the table, all at the same time.

Her behavior and actions really made me angry, and I struggled to maintain my composure. I lowered my voice, made direct eye contact, and firmly requested that she lessen up her grip on me. I was not smiling when I spoke to her, and her eyes grew very wide. However, she was like a dog with a bone. She obviously figured that since she had me, she was going to get her money's worth.

I did try to act as professional as possible while she squashed my fingers. I informed her that my personal religious views had nothing to do with my abilities as a reader and that contacting her mother was not like just looking up someone in a "book of the dead" type of phone book.

While I fought a short battle with my temper, a flood of psychic information came to me. No matter who you are, when any strong emotion is involved with psychic abilities, the volume tends to be turned up. So if you are angry, frustrated, or upset, expect the psi abilities to be turned up to full blast.

I had never been angry with a client before, and that day to my surprise I discovered that when my temper was loose, the psychic information came stronger and faster than it ever had before. I took a deep breath and tried to stay calm and let the intense psychic information from the rude client wash right into me. More by accident than design, I remember closing my eyes and thinking, *Okay, anybody out there in the afterlife who has something to say and is connected to this woman?*

Immediately I got a visual impression of an older couple standing arm in arm in front of a house in the suburbs. I realized I was looking at the past by the style of clothes they were wearing and because there was a

1950s-era car next to them. The couple was laughing so hard that they were wiping tears off their faces. I also picked up on the information that they felt like relatives. Then I heard in my mind the words *aunt* and *uncle*.

What came through from the couple was, *She always was demanding, dear. Don't take it personally.*

That shocked me. I was used to seeing a client's memories, which would technically be called a postcognitive experience by clairvoyant ability, but I had never had the memories actually talk back or interact with me. Holy crap!

I felt a warmth come from the couple—there was a real physical presence here—and it actually felt like a hug. I was stunned. Quickly, before I lost the contact, I asked them in my mind, *Show me something so I can tell her.*

They chuckled and suddenly I was seeing a child falling down, and then the same child was standing there with a cast on her arm. Then they showed me the older car that was sitting in the driveway next to them. The entire time the couple stood arm in arm; obviously they were a tight unit even in the afterlife. They radiated warmth and love. It was amazing.

As they smiled at me, I saw the man wink as they showed me their niece's adventure when she had stayed with them many years ago. I started to chuckle myself. This couple had such a sense of fun about them. What they were showing me was a bit difficult to make sense of at first, so I started telling the client what I was picking up before I lost the connection. I described what I was seeing and asked if this was familiar to her. The client flinched, dropped my hand, then started to laugh helplessly.

Turns out when the client was a little girl, she had stayed for the weekend with her aunt and uncle. She had been playing in their car, which was parked in the driveway, and somehow she knocked the car out of gear. Then she fell out of the open car door onto the driveway and broke her arm. Apparently her mother was furious that it had happened while she was in her relatives' care. However, that story of "remember the time you fell out of the car and broke your arm?" was apparently a family favorite.

While my client laughed until she cried over her aunt and uncle paying her a visit, in my mind I saw them wave goodbye and heard them tell me *thank you*. I took note that they sounded far away and distorted, like they were underwater or something. That distortion of sound made it difficult for me to understand everything they said. This made me wonder if it was the reason I have a harder time with clairaudience. Hmmm. Very interesting.

That was the first time I ever had what I assumed was someone else's memory talk back to me. Turns out it wasn't a memory at all. There was a real personality there, a very loving and humorous presence. It was then I realized I had just had my first true mediumship experience.

So what caused my postcognitive reading to roll into a medium-style one? Temper. Getting good and angry that day made me forget not to look too deep. While I would usually be very careful about how much I allowed myself to see when I held a client's hand, being angry at the client rudely squeezing my hand and pulling me across the table turned the tide.

Those first presences that came through for me were humorous and gave both the client and me a good chuckle. I will always remember that reading fondly—not because I got manhandled by a client but because the first folks I contacted on the other side were lovely, warm, and downright funny. The best lessons are often learned in the most unusual ways.

Oh, Crap! I Can Talk to Dead People? Getting Down to the Mechanics

As time passed, I practiced my mediumship abilities when the opportunity presented itself. As my ability grew, I researched more to see how exactly this worked for other people. And as I stated in the introduction, that search for information was a bust. I did not want to wade through other folks' religious beliefs. What I wanted was the mechanics.

Also, I want to point out at this time why I use the terminology that I do. I typically refer to the people or personalities whom I encounter from the other side while performing mediumship readings as "presences." I do this to differentiate between a ghost or spirit that is bound to the physical plane, such as in a haunting. The presences I do connect with during a medium-style reading are not here on the earthly plane. A medium works as a bridge from our physical plane to the other realm, or afterworld.

These are the steps for a medium-style reading:

- first ask permission to touch the client's hand

- hold the client's hand

- close your eyes and slow down your breathing

- ground and center your own personal energy

- shift your attention to your third eye area

- feel the person's hand in yours and make the psychic link by using clairtangency

- wait for that inner click or a spontaneous cognitive pop and see what you experience postcognitively

- allow the psychic information to roll in; you might psychically see, feel, know, or hear

- relay the information to the client

- if you get a hit on a real presence, silently ask how that presence is linked to the client

- gather information (images, names, emotions, knowledge) from that presence to relay to the client

- look around the presence—did they bring anyone along?

- when that presence and you are finished talking, silently say thank you and encourage the visiting presence to return to the other side and be at peace

That's the nuts and bolts; the rest is just ability and practice—lots and lots of practice.

As time passed, I started to challenge myself. Soon I was able to do medium-style readings without having to kickstart the process by using clairtangency, or psychic touch. It was like once I learned the mental pathway, it became easier and more familiar each time I traveled down it.

One of the more interesting things I have discovered is that your own personality creates the tone of a medium-style reading. By this I mean that the kind of individual you are colors the type of medium reading you will do and what sort of characters you attract from the other side. For example, I use humor when I write and teach. I'm funny, and I always have been. I can say that without ego. Furthermore, family is vitally important to me, and I tend to connect with folks on the other side who have a strong sense of love for their living family and a damn fine sense of humor.

Often these presences find a very comical way to get my attention. I can't count the number of times over the years I have had to say to clients, "Wow, this is going to sound really weird, but do you understand what (insert an odd or random image here) means?"

I don't know if I am relieved or tickled when that gets a big gasp and then a laugh from the clients as they recognize whatever random thing the presence from the other side is waving at me. Truthfully, if clients start to laugh, they will relax—and that allows me to get "in" deeper and to get better, clearer information while I am reading for them.

Because of this, when I do a medium-style reading, they tend to be warmer; the information I share typically is focused on the clients' family or closest friends. It makes the clients laugh and feel good. Sure, there are often tears, as connecting with someone who has passed away is always emotional, but there is love and laughter too.

That is very important to me as a psychic and as a human being in general. During a medium-style reading, if you lead with love and share some laughter with a client, you will always have a winning combination.

Medium-Style Readings in a Crowd: Are We Having Fun or What?

Let's say you already feel pretty confident as a medium and you are ready and raring to try your hand at reading for a crowd, just like the mediums on television do. If you have visions of reality TV glory…hold on there, partner. Medium-style readings are never about making yourself look good, nor are they to be attempted in a bid for fame and fortune. If you start down that ego-motivated slope, I can tell you right now that you will only self-destruct.

As a medium, your goal is to share information with your client. You are there to help them find closure, to aid them in working constructively through the grieving process, and most of all to assist their emotional healing. You cannot perform mediumship effectively when personal ego is involved.

Emotions will run high when you perform medium-style readings. Expect it and mentally prepare for it; consider carefully the ramifications of what you tell your client. Here is yet another reason why I employ humor with medium-style readings: laughter is healing. Be kind and compassionate. Medium-style readings are only to be done for the benefit of others and in a manner that harms no one.

Here is something else to contemplate. When you do medium-style readings in a crowd, you had better bring your "A" game, my friend. By this, I mean that in your repertoire you should have the patience of a saint, the humor of a stand-up comedian, and the steely nerves of a middle-school physical education teacher—because you never know who or what you are going to pick up on.

Here is a bit of information that most professional psychics and mediums won't share: doing medium-style readings in a room filled with people who are all focused on you is a cake walk! All you have to do is use your own energy and reach out to find the strongest and most compatible psychic energy (as in the easiest person to link to).

Take a good look at the folks in the room. You will recognize the easiest read when you see them. You might know them by sight (clairvoyance). If you are clairaudient, then you may hear your inner voice say, "That one." Or you'll identify them by the way they make you feel (clairsentience), or you may simply "just know" by claircognizance/intuition which energy you are the most psychically attracted to. Once you have connected to their energy, focus on them and let their postcognitive experiences roll in. Try using the steps outlined previously.

Typically the easiest medium-style read from a crowd is often someone who is open, excited, and curious. Or, perversely, if you have a skeptic in the group, they can be radiating such loud psychic information that you will pick up on them anyway. This falls into the category of "methinks thou dost protest too much." Sometimes the biggest skeptics are the most desperate to be proven wrong, so don't be surprised if you find yourself drawn to them.

The other interesting thing that can happen while doing medium-style readings in a crowd is that you may also pull in information from the people sitting next to the individual you are reading for. These other folks may have no connection to the person you are actually reading for other than their physical proximity to each other and that they came to the same event. Let me show you what I mean...

A Funny Thing Happened on the Way to the Group Reading...

Last year I was on tour and lecturing on psychic abilities—specifically on how to perform readings for the public. The lecture covered tarot and psychic readings for difficult clients, information on the ethics of mediumship, and a demonstration of a medium-style reading for someone in the crowd.

That day, there had been one middle-aged gentleman in the crowd who kept direct eye contact with me the entire lecture. His wife was captivated by the talk, but it was very obvious to me that he was only along to humor the wife. He rolled his eyes at me and smirked so many times that I started to get annoyed. However, there would be no showing off or rubbing the skeptic's nose in it just because I could, so I blocked him out as best as I could.

When the time came for the mediumship demonstration, I reached out for the most compatible and easiest energy to read. As I walked into the rows where the crowd was seated, I happened to move closer to the skeptic, who was sitting on the aisle.

As I reached out energetically, I hit immediately on the fact that the skeptic's father had passed away a year before. *Nope, not going there*, I thought. So I ignored him and kept searching.

It didn't do any good. I argued silently with myself and kept searching for a better person to read, and wouldn't you just know it? The tug I felt toward this gentleman was very strong—too strong to be ignored. Perfect, I had to be drawn to the skeptic. Sometimes being a medium is a ginormous pain in the ass.

Mentally I sighed, psyched myself up, and then made direct eye contact with the man. He responded by smiling and sitting up at attention. Well, at least he was curious. When he smiled, I felt that inner click. *Gotcha*, I thought to myself. I politely asked for his name; we will call him Ralph for the purpose of this story.

I said to Ralph, "I am going to ask you some questions in this reading, and I want yes or no answers, or very specific short ones. Do you understand?" Ralph agreed, and his wife squealed in excitement.

"Go ahead," he invited me and then added, "I don't believe in this stuff anyway." He then linked his arms behind his head and leaned back in the chair, as if to illustrate just how much he didn't. While his wife sputtered in embarrassment, I continued to study Ralph.

He was bluffing. I could feel with my clairsentience/psychic empathy that he was hurting over the loss of his father, and this attitude was simply a front to cover his hurt. Then I heard someone in the crowd make a comment about this being an excellent demonstration of reading for difficult people. The crowd chuckled a bit, and Ralph just sat back and gave me an I-dare-you look.

The more I studied Ralph, the harder a pull came from the other side. Definitely male, and it definitely felt paternal. This must be Ralph's dad. In my mind I asked the presence to be patient, and I would get to his son for him. In response I felt a little burst of warmth. *Here we go,* I thought to myself.

"You lost your father this past year." I didn't question Ralph. I stated it as a fact.

"Yes, I did," he admitted, and he wasn't smirking anymore. The crowd in the lecture hall went quiet.

I wasted no time in gloating. I got down to business. I began by describing the presence that I sensed and saw, then I asked him if his father had brothers on the other side with him. I told him the name of one of his uncles. Now Ralph sat up very straight in his chair and kept his eyes glued to me.

I was having trouble getting his father's name. While I could describe his coloring, build, and personality, and did so for Ralph, for clarity I asked for his father's name. Once I got the name (we'll call Ralph's father George), the real barrage of psychic information started.

I told Ralph that his dad was showing me many different hats. He would take one off and put another one on. Then George's presence tipped me a wink and called me Toots.

I relayed this to Ralph, and his wife began to cry. Apparently George had called Ralph's wife that. I asked Ralph if his dad was a "man of many hats" or had held lots of different jobs in his lifetime or something, because George just kept showing me more and more different types of hats—cowboy, fedora, baseball, you name it—and I was getting very confused.

Ralph said to me that the "many hats" thing was wrong. Then he crossed his arms over his chest defensively and shut down. No more help from that quarter. Ralph admitted I had nailed everything else, but the hat thing made no sense. I was stumped for a moment, and then the presence of George gave me a nudge and brought a young man forward with him. I got the impression the young man needed help from someone to communicate. To me that meant he was brand-new on the other side.

So I stopped and switched my focus to this new presence. Now I had to be very careful and find all my reserves of tact. Very carefully, and as gently as possible, I asked Ralph's wife if they had recently lost a young man in their family. He would have been a teenager, I explained, and his passing was very recent—as in a week or so ago. She shook her head no, and Ralph tossed up his hands in disgust.

I closed my eyes and focused on that younger presence again. Sure enough, George had his arm around the figure of a young man, and as they moved closer to me I saw that the young man was in a suit, and he kept pointing to his hair and smiling—like there was something on the side of his head. I got the impression of a design shaved into his hair. The young man's presence was radiant, and my breath caught at how peaceful and happy he was.

I knew I was right about Ralph's dad, so what the hell was happening here? Well, the truth is that old George of the many hats *was* acting as a guide, but who he was guiding was a mystery.

Then a quiet female voice spoke up from the crowd. "Excuse me?" she waved at me. "I think you may be describing my nephew," she said with a wobbly smile. She was sitting right next to Ralph the skeptic's wife.

"Only tell me your nephew's first name," I said to her.

She supplied the first name of her nephew, and I silently asked the presence if this was his name. He smiled and connected to me firmly, while Ralph's father's presence moved back. I looked at the woman and told her what I saw about the suit and his hair.

She started to cry as she explained that he did indeed have a pattern shaved into his hair. Then the younger man pointed to his head again, and I felt a sharp pain. I carefully told the woman what I was seeing and feeling. She confirmed that her nephew had been a victim of a random drive-by shooting. He had been struck in the head. He was only sixteen when he died. They had buried him in his brand-new suit the week before.

The young man's presence shared some more information with me, and I started to chuckle a bit as he showed me a big hairy-looking mutt that was by his side. I actually smelled that wet dog smell. The dog was shedding hair all over the boy's suit too. I shared this information with the aunt.

Turns out that this big goofy dog had been a beloved family pet that had passed away a year ago. The boy's aunt started to laugh and informed me that no matter how much they had bathed that dog he had always smelled, and they were still finding dog hair a year later. She was touched that the dog was there with him. I told her that the young man was requesting that his aunt pass the information from the reading to his mother, and also to tell his mom that he loved her, that he was fine, and that he was not alone.

Then the dog, the young man, and Ralph's father moved back. I silently wished them well and thanked them. Now that the room was quiet, I explained to the crowd that sometimes when you have folks sitting together, their combined energy brings more than one presence to a place where I can talk to them.

I was wrapping up the lecture when unexpectedly Ralph shot his hand up in the air and interrupted me with a sudden thought. "My father had a hat collection! I was just going through it yesterday, trying to decide what to keep and what to toss. Oh my God, could that be the 'many different hats' that you saw?" he asked incredulously.

I kept a straight face and replied, "Absolutely. *Many. Hats. Hat collection.* That explains it." A few folks around him were starting to chuckle. I tried to keep from sounding frustrated as I continued with, "That was your father's way of getting my attention—so I could share with you something that would prove to you it was really him."

The crowd lost it. Everyone started to chuckle. Ralph started to laugh himself, and I noticed that his wife had her arm around the woman next to her—the aunt of the young man George's presence had guided in. Those people had never met before, but their relatives had banded together to get a message through from the other side.

See what I mean about the patience of a saint? Sometimes you will want to slam your head against the wall in frustration when folks don't get the clues the presence from the other side is relaying to you for them. But before you go all superior thinking how much smarter you are, stop. Remember that in a medium-style reading you are putting that person on the spot. They might panic and not think about what you are saying.

Half the time they are going to wonder if you are on the level, or they might get too excited or emotional from the information you share. You have them at a disadvantage, and they often draw blanks in the heat of the moment. So try your best to be patient. Always be compassionate, and remember that a touch of humor can lighten up even difficult situations nicely.

Lastly, Consider This…

Please remember that as a medium, your own personality dictates who you will best connect with. I stated this earlier, but it is worth repeating. Also, it is important to realize that you will not always get the party on the other side that your client requests because your energy may simply not be compatible with the individual who has passed over. That may be tough to hear, but you would do well to remember that. You are not omnipotent. Do not promise a client that you can reach whichever loved ones they wish for. Sometimes the person they want to communicate with is not who they really need.

Once you have made contact, then it is up to you to screen that presence. Think about it. We do not share our personal information with random strangers in the regular course of our days. Some people rub you the wrong way or you take an instant dislike to them. You also would not force a stranger to communicate with you either. The same commonsense behavior should be applied to presences on the other side.

Be smart and follow your instincts. If the presence feels wrong to you, then refuse to communicate with it. I know it's okay if I get a warm burst of energy from them. It's a warm rush and feels like a little hug or a friendly hip bump. Also, I do not open myself up from a position of weakness. No, indeed. I stand tall and proud, and put out a vibe that lets the other side know I will not tolerate any nonsense. It is like an energetic version of the look I can still give to my grown children that makes both of my over-six-foot-tall sons cringe a bit. It's the don't-even-think-about-it, hands-on-your-hips type of energy. You know the Warrior Mom look? That's the one. Loving but firm.

While doing a medium-style reading, you should stand strong and then request politely if there are any loved ones on the other side who are connected to the client. Always be polite. Manners count here, people. Ask gently if they would like to come forward at this time, then see who comes forward. If the energy seems correct to you, and you are comfortable, then you can proceed.

I want to take a moment here and state that it is not unusual to get impressions of pets that have passed over too. Watch for them when you make contact with a client's loved one. The presence of the pet won't speak to you, but they will show you their personality and physical traits. They are sort of secondary characters. I have found that information about the departed pets of the people who have passed over are a way of providing validation to a client.

Also, you should be aware that there is a bit of a timing issue to deal with when it comes to medium-style readings. I quickly found out that there seems to be a "dead space" of time (I'm not being insensitive here— that's the best way to describe it) after someone passes away. Typically it takes an individual six months to a year to adjust to being on the other side before you can easily contact them. I think of this as an adjustment period for those folks, where they get their bearings and become used to their afterlife. Then if they are so inclined and your energy is compatible with theirs, they can choose to come forward.

That's right: *they choose.* You do not force them (the presence of the departed) to communicate with you. It is up to them, so keep that in mind. Otherwise you would be the equivalent of a psychic bully.

Over the years I have had occasional exceptions to that general rule of six months to a year. One of them was the situation I just described, when one established presence helped bring another new presence forward and when the recently departed individual is desperate to get through to the client—not the other way around.

I once was doing a quick tarot reading for a client and a presence started talking to me. I heard them crystal clear; as clairaudience is something I often have trouble discerning, it slammed me to a stop. I am sure it looked pretty strange to the woman and her friends who insisted on sitting in on her tarot reading to have me stop mid-sentence and just sit there with my head cocked to one side while I listened.

In this case, the presence on the other side was desperate to tell his friend that it was not her fault that he had committed suicide. Oh boy, that was not an easy message to relay. The presence was determined to let her know that she was not at fault, and he insisted to me that he could not go forward fully into his afterlife until he straightened this out. Apparently her misplaced guilt was upsetting him, and he wanted her to be at peace and stop blaming herself. This was a presence who desperately wanted to find a resolution.

That was a tough conversation. I had to be very gentle with the client, who felt if only she would have checked on him an hour earlier she could have stopped him. At first she thought her friends who were sitting in on the reading had set her up. Then I was able to relay several funny anecdotes to her from the recently departed friend that only she would know about. That presence kept at it, with one funny story after another, until she stopped crying.

The moment she realized the truth and said out loud, "It really wasn't my fault; he wanted to go," he stepped back and was gone. That was one hell of a day, I have to admit.

In a rare situation like this, you can get the feeling that as a medium, you are more or less along for the ride. However, it is my opinion that if you have medium abilities, then you had better toughen up. There is no such thing as a free lunch. A medium who has psychically opened up even for a typical tarot reading needs to be aware that occasionally a determined presence can use you to relay a message. It is unusual, but sometimes it does happen.

Sure, there are plenty of times when I am doing a tarot reading when I feel a presence pushing at me. I can choose to ignore them or communicate with them. It is rare to have one break through with no warning. I have found that when this happens, it is always for a good reason; each time it has happened to me, it ending up bringing both healing and peace to the client, which only proves that love is the most unstoppable force in the universe. And at the end of the day, I can live with being the messenger from one loved one to another.

Chapter 5

Tarot Cards: Tools of the Psychic's Trade

When the average person thinks of psychics, they think of tarot cards. I will be the first to admit that tarot cards do have a romantic sort of mystique. You know how it goes—the mysterious woman wearing a colorful scarf over her tumbling hair beckons the client into a smoky room. The room is only illuminated by flickering candlelight, and many rings flash on her fingers as the fortuneteller gestures with her outstretched hand. The client is drawn forward in fascination and sits at her draped table. Fragrant incense smoke curls toward the ceiling as she picks up a battered, well-used tarot deck and shuffles the cards. She quickly lays a complicated spread of tarot cards down upon her reading table. As the client looks from the cards to the fortuneteller, they realize that within her eyes lie all of the mysteries of the universe…

"I know why you are here," the tarot reader announces in a smoky voice.

Or something like that. Honestly, I have met as many male psychics as female, so perhaps we need to adjust that overly romantic perception of the fortuneteller and take a look at the reality of the tools of the trade. Tarot cards are not strictly necessary for psychic readings; however, they are traditional tools, and they are a lot of fun to work with.

The tarot is a deck of seventy-eight mystical cards that has been used for centuries as a divinatory tool. No one really knows for sure how it began, who invented it, or when tarot first appeared. The debate on the topic of the tarot's origins could fill up a book alone. The least that you need to know is that in 1909 Golden Dawn members Arthur Edward Waite and Pamela Colman Smith developed the well-known Rider-Waite deck. As the deck was originally published by the Rider Company, it became popularly known as the Rider-Waite Tarot. However, in recent years an effort to acknowledge the artist's talents has emerged, so today the deck is properly referred to as the Rider-Waite-Smith deck. This is the standard deck, especially in the United States. Also, the majority of tarot decks that are published these days are typically based on the setup and style of the Rider-Waite-Smith deck.

A tarot deck is classically made up of twenty-two major arcana cards and fifty-six minor arcana cards, divided into four suits. The sequence of the major arcana's twenty-two cards tells us the story of the Fool's journey. The Fool is an archetype that represents each of us. He is the everyman, and this is illustrated by being the first card in the major arcana. From this starting point as a card numbered zero, we see this traveler begin his quest. He is young, carefree, happy, and open to the experiences of his spiritual passage. By the time the Fool works his way through to the final major arcana card, numbered twenty-one and entitled the World, our spiritual traveler is older, wiser, and has embraced the mysteries of his life's path.

What is fascinating is that the word *arcana* actually means "mystery." The scenes in the twenty-two major arcana cards show us evocative images and archetypes. These archetypes are symbolic figures such as the Traveler or the Seeker, the Mother, the Father, the High Priest and High Priestess, and the Hero. These archetypal images are drawn from many mystical cultures and appear in various mythologies, religions, and mystery traditions from all over the world. They are truly universal. At any point in our lives we can embody a major arcana card and feel as if we are living with the scene itself. These particular twenty-two cards appeal to our emotions and tug on our heartstrings. The imagery and archetypes within the major arcana link us all together as they resonate on a deeper spiritual level. They speak to us by using the common language of emotion.

When major arcana cards turn up in a tarot spread, they add weight and importance to the reading. These cards illustrate important spiritual matters and reveal our relationship to the particular archetype within the card. When two or more major arcana cards are dealt in a reading, then you know that fate is playing a hand in your spiritual path and everyday life. Take comfort in that, as these major arcana cards teach you that while things may seem beyond your control, there is a divine and mystical purpose at work here.

The minor arcana consists of four different suits: cups, swords, wands, and pentacles. Each of these suits aligns with one of the four natural elements. The suits of wands and swords are considered to have masculine, active energies assigned to their elemental rulers of fire and air. The suits of cups and pentacles are feminine, passive energies aligned with water and earth. It is also interesting to note that in readings the suits of pentacles (earth) and wands (fire) represent physical activities, while the suits of cups (water) and swords (air) symbolize the emotions that are being felt. The different elements characterize not only different experiences but also very different ways of approaching the challenges in your life.

Also, in regard to the minor arcana and within each of the four suits, there are two different sets of cards. To begin, we have the pips, or numbered cards: the ace through ten. The second set of cards in the minor arcana are the court cards, including the page, knight, queen, and king of each suit. The court cards classically represent the real people and personalities that you have to interact with in your life.

In closing, the minor arcana—both pip and court cards—shows us the everyday, ordinary situations and personalities that we deal with and face in our lives. The minor arcana cards bring meaning to events, clarity to the challenges we face, and provide illumination to the common questions we ask.

How Does the Tarot Deck Work?

There are many theories as to how exactly the tarot deck works. Personally, I believe it is a combination of symbolism, synchronicity, and a personal interconnectedness. Everything and everyone in the universe is connected on some level—energetically, spiritually, or through a type of personal compatibility. Also, there is and has always been a divine connection between your psychic awareness and those future possibilities. A tarot deck allows you one way to visually explore this connection.

The images and scenes portrayed in the cards are there to give you a starting point, but it is up to you and your intuition to interpret the cards. Tarot cards are wonderful tools that will allow you deeper access into the psychic realm, as every individual image portrayed in the scene of a single tarot card is there for a specific reason. Symbolism is the language of the tarot, and each card tells its own wonderful story. I encourage you to look carefully at each card in your own tarot deck, learn their classic meanings, and then take it further and see what tales the cards tell and what lessons they teach as you work with them.

Think of your tarot deck as a springboard. The symbolism in the cards is your jumping-off point. Adding your intuition and whatever other types of psychic abilities you possess to your readings will give your readings depth and texture. Remember that when the cards are dealt, it shows you the energy of the moment and what is the most important information to be acknowledged for the client. (There's that synchronicity at work for you.) It is essential to work with the energy that is present when the cards are dealt so you can see the future in clearer detail.

I have always thought of tarot readings like signposts on a road. As the client travels down the road of life (or you might like to think of this as a personal path), they can choose to heed the signposts along their journey or ignore them. These signposts only show possibilities and may confirm things from the client's subconscious that they may or may not have realized or accepted. Perhaps by heeding the signposts that are revealed during a tarot reading, they may choose to travel down a completely new path—or they may continue down their current route with a new awareness and understanding of how to best deal with any future events or situations.

By sharing the information or pointing out the psychic landscape and the signs along the way during a tarot reading, you are basically offering the client travel options. Just remember that you are a guide, not a conductor. You may suggest and point out the scenery, so to speak, but how they get there is up to them. What the clients choose to do with the information or what path they ultimately choose to travel is, of course, completely up to them.

Performing a Tarot Reading for Another

Now, when it comes to performing a reading for another, there are some rules you should consider.

Ask If the Client Has Ever Had a Reading Before

If not, then take that opportunity to explain what some of the more intense tarot images actually symbolize. This way you avoid any frights or upsets from the client. For example, the Ten of Swords symbolizes being betrayed or "stabbed in the back," while the Death card actually shows change. (The Death card typically pops up in readings for pregnant women or people about to get married or head off to college, etc. After all, their life is about to change forever in a big way.) Another card that unnecessarily upsets folks is the Devil card. As a matter of fact, when I scripted my own tarot deck, I replaced that card with a completely different title. I called it "The Shadow Side." However, the meaning for this major arcana card is basically the same: this fifteenth major arcana card means that you feel trapped and are dealing with people whom you cannot please, such as the relative from hell or a sociopathic boss. This card also states that you have given away your personal power, and it urges you to "cowboy up" and face your fears... And when you explain it that way to a client ahead of time, they are prepared, empowered, and engaged. So stop and give the client some reassurance before their very first reading begins. That way you can both enjoy the experience.

Ask the Client What Specific Question They Have or If This Is an "Overview" Type of Reading at the Start

Have them hold the question firmly in mind while they shuffle the cards. Yes, your tarot deck may be handled by someone else. It is best to have the client shuffle and cut the deck themselves before the reading; that way, their energy and actions influence the cards and how they fall. There are some people who insist that you should never let another person handle your cards. (Which is a tough trick to pull off when you are doing a reading for someone else.) An easy solution to this dilemma is that if you are doing readings for the public, then you may want a separate deck strictly dedicated for public readings and another set of cards just for your own personal use.

You Do Not Have to Read Reversed Cards—Unless You'd Like To

I rarely do. Life is full of enough challenges. Besides, it does occasionally upset folks when they see upside-down cards. Whether or not you decide to read reversed cards is your personal choice.

Never Predict Death

Odds are that you are wrong. Worse, what if you are wrong and someone decides to take you up on your prediction? In all the years I have done readings, I can count the number of times on one hand that the cards actually predicted imminent physical death, and each time it was in conjunction with someone inquiring about a relative who was in their final days, battling an illness of some kind.

Know Your Deck

It really kills the mood and makes you look unprofessional if you have to stop and look up the answers in the book during a public reading. So if you are doing readings for the public, then know the deck cold. When I first started working with a tarot deck, I chose three or four keywords for each card and then memorized those suckers, which worked for me. I recommend to any new tarot students I work with today to do the same. It is very much worth your time if you plan to read professionally, which rolls into the second part of this: be sure to take some time to practice before you read for the general public. Practice for your friends and relatives, then practice on their friends, then practice some more.

Storing Your Tarot Cards

Finally, when you are all through with your reading, your tarot cards do *not* have to be wrapped in or stored in silk. The reason this folklore began is that silk deflects unwanted psychic vibrations, but this is not strictly necessary. If the idea appeals to you, then go for it. I typically place my tarot cards in a drawstring fabric pouch. It keeps them clean and together, and it makes it harder to lose a card. I have different fabrics and various color drawstring bags for my different decks so I can tell them apart quickly.

It Is Okay to Laugh and Have Fun with a Tarot Reading

It is also perfectly fine to be more serious and thoughtful. Again, your personal style and your choice should be honored. We are all unique, and that difference gives our tarot readings personality and depth.

Tarot Card Spreads for You to Try

Reading tarot cards is not hard, but many people freeze when it comes down to actually performing a reading for another. So your best bet is to keep it simple by using uncomplicated spreads. There are many varieties of spreads, which is a good thing, as it allows for some personalization and freedom while doing your readings. I have found over the years that it is best to find one card spread that works for you and then stick with that. The longer you use the same spread, the more you begin to learn what it means for you personally as a reader when a specific card falls in a particular position. What you need to remember is this: the pattern that the cards are laid out in provides the structure for any reading.

Here are a few classic spreads, such as a single-card reading, a three-card reading, and the seven-card spread called the Horseshoe.

One-Card Reading

I like single-card readings. They are short, sweet, and to the point. A few months ago I did them for the people standing in line at an event where I was signing my books and my tarot deck. As people stood in line, working their way down the row to all of the various authors in attendance, one woman was eyeballing my tarot deck pretty hard. I smiled at her and invited her to look through the deck if she liked. She frowned at me and said that she didn't believe in the tarot. I asked her if she'd ever had a reading before, and she sniffed, tossed her head, and informed me that she hadn't. I smiled at her and invited her to choose one card. Her friends in line encouraged her to try it.

I tried to look particularly nonthreatening and informed her with a cheeky grin that I hadn't bitten anyone all day. She chuckled and with a what-the-hell attitude chose a card at random out of the deck that lay face down and stacked neatly on the signing table. She picked up the Hermit card. I smiled up at her and then quickly explained the definition of the card. Basically I told her that she needed some alone time to think things over and take a bit of a break. I informed her that the answers to the question she was struggling with were to be found by looking within. She jolted, admitted that I was right on the money, and handed me the card back while her friends howled with laughter. I only smiled and gently reminded her that she had chosen the card herself.

One-card readings are powerful, as they cut straight to the heart of the matter. Shuffle the deck and then fan the cards out face down, across the table. Now have the client ask themselves, "What is it that I most need to know?" Then have them choose one card. They may choose to hold their dominant hand (the one they write with) out over the cards and see which one feels right or they can simply choose one at random out of a stacked deck.

Another good tip is that one-card readings are great ways to do readings for yourself. A single-card reading is also a nice way to get a handle on whatever lessons your day may hold. Shuffle the deck. Ask for your hands to be guided and for the wisdom to help you comprehend the message, and pull out one card.

Other good questions for a one-card reading for yourself include:

- "What is my personal lesson for the day?"
- "Is there a message for me from Spirit today?"
- "What is hidden from me?"
- "Where should I focus my talents?"

This is also fun type of reading to do at a gathering. Simply have each person pull one card and pass the deck around clockwise. After everyone has drawn a card, have them look together at their cards, then discuss the meanings and talk about the cards.

Three-Card Reading

Three-card readings are fun. Many tarot readers use a three-card layout for quick or mini readings. There are many variations on how you may interpret a trinity of cards. You start by dealing the cards out in a horizontal line from left to right. One of the most common three-card spread patterns is as follows:

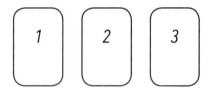

1) past

2) present

3) future

When divining the answer to a problem or problematic situation, you can use this interpretation, where the three card positions are defined as follows:

1) what is unknown about the current problem

2) what is blocking you

3) how to proceed for best results

When you first begin working with tarot cards, I would recommend using a simple three-card spread. As your confidence grows, then move up to the Horseshoe Spread.

Seven-Card Horseshoe Spread

Without a doubt, the seven-card reading is my favorite style of tarot reading. I prefer this structure of card layouts over all others. What is nice about this reading is that you can layer another set of cards over the first. This gives you a deeper meaning and provides more insight into a reading for another. Shuffle the cards well and ask your question. Deal out seven cards from left to right. Now take a careful look at the cards that appear in your reading.

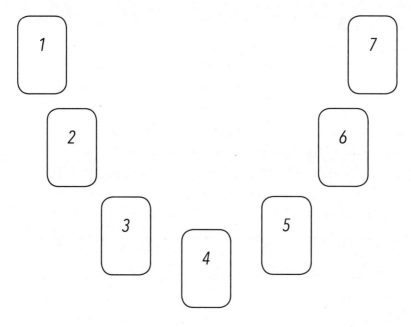

- The first card of the reading will signify the past and what brought you to this point.

- The second card is the present, meaning what is happening right now.

- The third card shows the future or what is yet to be.

- The fourth card represents your best course of action or the best way for you to proceed.

- The fifth card represents the other people in the situation: who they are, what motivates them, and how they affect your life.

- The sixth card signifies your obstacles and fears.

- The seventh and final card is the outcome card.

I think that about covers the basics. Learning a tarot deck takes a long time; do not rush the process. Slow down and learn at your own pace. Enjoy yourself and remember that practice does indeed make perfect.

Survival Guides for Tarot Readers and Psychics

Here is what you need to know when you perform tarot readings and psychic readings for the general public. You may think some of this is common sense, but it has been my experience that common sense isn't always very common. These are all pointers I wish someone would have shared with me before I started doing readings for the public. Truthfully, very few folks talk about the challenges and the interesting characters you will encounter. I find it worth the time to go over some survival scenarios. So tuck your tongue firmly in your cheek and get ready for some real-life information.

Be Discreet

You are going to be learning personal, private things about the people you read for. You should never gossip about your clients to friends, family, or other clients. If you want to build and maintain a good reputation, then you need to be discreet.

That being said, brace yourself. There are people out there who are going to tell you some truly wild stuff. Some folks will confide in you about their extramarital affairs, the lies they tell, and their deepest fears when they look for guidance or for their bad behavior to be validated. I think sometimes those individuals figure that if you are a psychic, then nothing should faze you.

Be Prepared for Weird

There, I said it, and you know what? I'm going to stand by that statement. I would love to sit here and tell you that only enlightened and emotionally balanced souls will come into your world, ready to embrace the wisdom of the tarot and your superior interpretation of the mysteries that lie within, but honestly that is not going to happen. If you do not have a sense of humor, I strongly recommend that you develop one immediately! And if you do have a good sense of humor, then get ready to put to use. It just may help to keep you from wanting to bang your head against the reading table.

Do Your Best and Know You Won't Be Able to Help Everyone

Madame Zolta you are not. Do your best and don't be afraid to say "I don't know." Sometimes no matter how hard you try, you may not be able to get a perfect reading for a client. Worst-case scenario and you have a really disastrous reading where nothing goes right? Then refund the client their money and recommend a different psychic or tarot reader.

I leave the client's money in full view on the table until the reading is done. When we are all finished, then I tuck it away. In all my years I have only had to offer to return someone's money once. When this occurred, I sat back, took a deep breath in, and slowly blew it out. I rolled my shoulders and recommended another reader, and the client was so shocked by my honesty that she stayed put and we kept working. It ended up that I was pulling in information from the client's daughter, who was sitting in on her mother's reading. Oops. (I knew there was a wedding and a baby coming very quickly; seems the daughter had not confided in her mom that she was pregnant yet.) She finally admitted it and then we were able to continue going forward with her mother's reading. Boy, I bet they had an interesting conversation on their car ride home.

Limit Your Client to One at a Time

(Which is the best way to avoid the scenario described just above.) It can be very confusing to have two, three, or four people sitting in close proximity to the client. Typically they are all leaning in and focused, so it's very easy to pick up on *all of them at the same time.* If they insist upon it, then I would gently but firmly tell them, with a smile, that the client deserves some privacy even if they are friends or family. Also warn them that you could pick up private and very personal information on any one of them should they insist upon sitting in the line of fire. That normally makes people laugh and scramble back from the reading table. If you get some diehards who refuse to leave, be sure to make them all sit back about five feet away from the table so your client has some privacy and you can stay focused on the client and not their posse.

Set Some Personal Boundaries

Learn how to say no. Do not give out your phone number to clients; otherwise they will call at all hours of the day and night. Do not give out your private email to clients. Been there, done that. If you want to be treated like a professional psychic/tarot reader, then you need to set some boundaries and stick to them. You are not a psychic drive-thru. You have the right to say no.

If you are tired or done for the day and someone comes in at the last minute or begs for more time when another client is waiting, you will have to set some limits and learn to say no. If I get someone who repeatedly plays the whole "Oh, but let me just ask one more thing," I scoop the cards off the table and then stand up. I thank them and tell them that our time is finished, and then I motion the next client over. Also, I have a hard limit on reading for the same person more than once every six months. There are obsessive folks/energy vampires who will just keep going to psychics over and over, trying to get the answer they want. Don't feed the addiction. Be polite but firm.

Protect Your Own Energy and Privacy

This expands on the previous point: there are some folks who feed off the rush of a psychic reading and your undivided attention like an unrepentant, uninvited energy vampire. The best protection is as suggested previously: learn to say no. Set boundaries. Do not become overly familiar with the energy vampire client. You'll know you have encountered one when they start asking you about your personal life, acting proprietary, or bringing gifts. You must understand that the kindest thing you can do in this situation is to shut them down. They see any opening as an invitation to take energy from you or try to establish some sort of personal relationship. Keep your personal friendships and your psychic/tarot clients separate. If this should become a problem, or the client becomes overly familiar, then simply and politely refuse to read for them anymore. This only becomes a drama if you allow it.

Take Breaks

You will need to take a break occasionally if you are performing many psychic or tarot readings back to back. I never do more than three readings back to back. In fact, if I am doing readings all day, then I schedule fifteen-minute breaks between blocks of three clients. At my break time I get up, move around, and typically go to the restroom where, whether I need to use the facilities or not, I always wash my hands. Not because I am a germaphobe but because the act of water pouring over my hands helps to break any lingering psychic links from my using clairtangency (psychic touch). Afterwards, when I head back to my table, I avoid getting caught by folks hanging around, hoping to hit me up for free psychic advice, by walking quickly and with purpose.

Once I am back at my table, I don't let a client just come in and sit and wait and chat. That probably makes me sound like a hard-ass, but I have my reasons. I insist upon a few moments of downtime, where I may powder my nose, reapply lipstick, or check my hair, and there is a very good reason for this. Whatever I do in my downtime between clients gives me some personal space and an opportunity to put the focus on myself and my own emotional and energetic well-being. I have learned that if I do not take a few moments to focus on myself and my own physical body, I might start carrying around unwanted psychic energy from the back-to-back readings. This downtime is yet another way to make an energetic and healthy break between myself and the psychic energy of all the clients. Boundaries: set them and stick to them.

Focus On Your Physical Body

Keep your protein levels up, drink plenty of water, and lay off the sugar! Bring water and snacks. You will need the water because you are going to be doing a lot of talking. Also, that water will help flush your system of any negativity the clients unknowingly bring in with them. When you get a break, eat something high in protein. Oh, and lay off the sugary foods! I know your body is craving that sugar, especially when you burn a lot of psychic and mental energy, but just like a person experiencing a blood sugar crash, remember that sugar and carbohydrates are the emergency rescue, not the cure. When someone's blood sugar goes dangerously low, they are given a sugary drink to yank their blood sugar levels up (rescue), then they eat something high in protein, which is the long-term remedy.

Protein is the long-term fix. Trust me. I battled hypoglycemia for years until I learned to change my diet. I know what I'm talking about, and I learned the hard way. Drinking a sugar-laden soft drink when your blood sugar levels dip would snap you back and give you a caffeine rush, but very shortly afterwards you will feel much worse. Protein bars are a fantastic and healthier option. They make vegan options too, and these days protein bars are readily available, portable, and discreet. I do prefer protein bars to a bag of mixed nuts as nut allergies are common and I will admit that I tend to end up spilling nuts all over the place. Just a little something to consider.

Keep these survival tips in mind, and you will be able to enjoy yourself when you perform those psychic or tarot readings. Experience is an excellent teacher, but there is no need to walk into situations being unprepared.

SOME PEOPLE ARE *far more*
cognizant than others, but sensitivity
has its own cross to bear…

Donna Lynn Hope

Chapter 6

Psychic Phenomena:
Psi-Sensitives, Ghost
Hunters, Séances &
SLIders

There is a big wide world of psychic phenomena out there. Over the years these are the topics I have been asked about the most often, so it really wasn't too hard for me to decide which types of psychic phenomena to write about.

The first topic I would like to discuss is sensitivity. When I say "sensitivity," I am speaking of those folks who have a psychic sensitivity, or psi-sensitivity for short. These folks pick up more information about their environment and the people around them than the average person. While a psi-sensitive may have an understanding that they are having a precognitive or postcognitive type of psychic experience, for a variety of reasons they may not link the experience together with an actual psychic ability.

There are many reasons for this. The first reason is, more often than not, fear. They are afraid of exploring their own talents. A psi-sensitive may also just shut down any ability they possess because they are unsure of how to process the information they are gathering, so they ignore it and refuse to acknowledge what they experience. Or they might have concerns that by exploring their own natural abilities, they are going to come into conflict with their own personal religion.

In case a reader has picked up this book and flipped to this section first before reading straight through from the beginning, allow me to illuminate you. Psychic abilities are a natural part of our lives. They are skills, talents, and innate abilities that are present in each and every one of us. Our religious affiliations have nothing to do with our psychic potential. Psychic abilities and experiences are a natural part of all humans, and there is nothing to be afraid of by exploring your own potential.

Now, the psi-sensitive is often a person holding a mixed bag of psychic abilities. However, for the psi-sensitive, the strongest ability is probably going to be clairsentience, or psychic empathy. Clairsentience means "clear feeling," after all—as in the feeling and gathering of psychic information from another person's emotions. Think about it: if these psi-sensitives are naturally sensitive, then they are going to be tuned in to other people's emotions and moods already, which is what makes them have empathy for others and causes them to be emotionally sensitive to begin with. What is fascinating to me about psi-sensitives is that they are typically unaware of just how much power they are carting around.

A psi-sensitive is typically a gentle soul; however, that gentleness is internal. Do not expect all psi-sensitives to be meek little mice and quiet librarian types who sit shyly in a corner. I have found over the years that psi-sensitive's personalities are as varied as the day is long. They might be the soft-spoken, serious type or they may have had to develop a sense of humor. Psi-sensitives can be witty, with a biting talent for sarcasm, or they can have a very gruff outer shell, which is needed to survive their extreme sensitivity to their own environment. Interestingly enough, some of the most talented psi-sensitives I have ever met were soldiers, police officers, detectives, paramedics, and nurses. There is something about this particular aptitude that often draws the psi-sensitive individual to a career that protects, serves, solves, rescues, and heals.

Some psi-sensitives do take up paranormal investigating as a hobby, and I ask you, who would be better? If I had to have a paranormal investigator or a detective come into my home, I would hope there would be a few psi-sensitives among the group because these folks would not only rely on their training, but they would also be paying attention to more subtle energetic information.

Psi-Sensitives vs. Mediums

It is important not to confuse a psi-sensitive with a medium. If you recall, I pointed out in chapter 4 that mediumship is an all-or-nothing psychic ability. It takes a specific type of talent to communicate with a presence from the other side and then be able to relay and interpret this information for a client.

A psi-sensitive, on the other hand, is sensitive to all types of energy both on the physical and the etheric planes. This includes ghosts, which are often thought to be spirits stuck in the physical world either accidentally or because they have unfinished business here in the physical realm. That knack for sensing what is often unseen to others is why psi-sensitives might be drawn to paranormal investigation. Where a medium would be communicating with a specific presence on the other side, a psi-sensitive, on the other hand, would be able to sense when a ghost was nearby and on the physical plane. They would know where to search, and they would sense this because they are a psi-sensitive using their psychic ability of clairsentience (psychic empathy). A psi-sensitive follows the trail of left-behind emotions like a postcognitive bloodhound on a scent. They go where the emotions are strongest and then this rolls into real psychic information that they can use and relay to their clients.

A psi-sensitive may experience precognition (psychic information about the future), but if they are investigating, they will be relying heavily on their postcognitive experiences, or psychic information about the past. As was discussed in the first chapter, postcognitive abilities come into play during a residual-style haunting. This is when the memories or emotions from a traumatic event have seeped into the location and left an emotional footprint. A psi-sensitive comes along and *ta-da!* They see, hear, or sense the energetic playback. If you feel that you are a psi-sensitive, then I suggest you go back and look at chapters 1 and 2 very carefully to figure out how your sensitivity manifests into information and into which specific psychic ability. Knowledge is power, and my goal with this book is for you to be empowered and informed.

What About Ghost Hunting and Paranormal Investigations?

Over the years I have had so many requests to either investigate or check out a haunted location that I have lost count. I rarely do this. I have turned down many offers to be a part of the local ghost-hunting groups, as the last thing I want to do is to have a chat with a wandering spirit. I avoid this not out of ego, but because being a mixed bag of psychic abilities *and* a medium makes the idea of being involved in lots of paranormal investigations less than an enjoyable prospect for me. The trouble is that ghost hunting is very popular these days. People want attention, and often the fastest way to get it is to announce that they think a dark or evil presence is lurking in the basement, behind the water heater, whether there is anything there or not.

There have been times where I have quietly taken a psychic look around a location at the request of the owner. In these cases I shared any postcognitive information I picked up privately with the building's owner and then suggested where I thought the best places for a future paranormal team to focus their efforts would be. Then I bow out. It is important to realize that not every psychic is a ghost hunter, nor should they be. If a situation arises that I am moved to check out, then I do so quietly. I prefer to handle these things privately, without getting a third party involved. I trust my own psychic abilities and my common sense to look into the history of a location before I'd trust a stranger from a group on the Internet.

Now before someone assumes from my tone that I do not approve of paranormal teams, that is simply not the case. Over the years I have met groups that were incredibly professional and dedicated. I have also met groups that were incredibly crazy and were convinced a reality television show was one haunted house away... I have also met a few "investigators" who were so full of themselves and their gadgets and toys that it was laughable.

However, if you are determined to have a group come in and investigate, then do some research. The toughest part is figuring out who is who and what their credentials actually are. If you go looking on the Internet, there are hundreds of paranormal groups in the United States alone. Your best option is to start looking for local groups and then talk to the folks who have worked with them. Ask those clients how were they treated, what they thought of the paranormal group, and so forth.

Or turn the tables and interview any prospective paranormal team first. They are going to want to interview you anyway to be sure *you* are on the level, so I suggest that you ask them some questions as well. Be sure to ask for references. Any group who is on the up-and-up will be happy to supply them. Be smart and take your time and know who you are dealing with before you discover that you have invited a bunch of strangers, all wearing neon-colored T-shirts with a ghostly insignia on them, to go traipsing through your house. Subtle.

I'd like to point out that a professional paranormal team would do the investigating for free. They should also be discreet, polite, and hopefully have no one singular religious affiliation so you can get an unbiased option and clear information. Wouldn't you rather have the investigators looking at a potential problem or haunting from a strictly scientific perspective or a multiviewed religious one? That way you have lots of options, and no one wants someone else's religious views being foisted on them. Good investigators should share information on what they find, not their own personal religious opinions. For example, the first time I ever came face-to-face with a real ghost, I then investigated the sighting from a nondenominational point of view. What I learned was fascinating.

No, Really, I Am *Not* a Ghostbuster!
(Or, Ellen Encounters a Ghost)

As a psychic, I do believe in the possibility of a ghost manifesting on the physical plane. However, I figured people were probably experiencing a postcognitive experience from an event in the past, but as I had never seen an actual ghostly figure "in the flesh," so to speak, I was a little skeptical of folks who said they saw a manifested figure of a person—full torso apparition and all that. That was for the movies, right?

In my past and varied career as a seasonally employed worker, waitress, and sales clerk, I have worked in several haunted locations during my life. My town is a river town, and it was founded in the 1700s, so we have lots of history and plenty of ghost stories. Once when I worked in the local historic district, I personally witnessed all of the silverware disappear from the famously haunted restaurant that I worked at. It all went right off the tables. I turned my back for a moment and all of it just vanished into thin air. All the waitstaff jumped as one when that happened. Unlike my fellow employees, I didn't panic; instead I laughed, got more utensils from the kitchen, and as calmly as possible reset the tables for the dinner shift.

The other servers didn't take it as well as I had. They were frightened and could not see the humor in it. Some of the employees wouldn't even go into certain rooms of the building by themselves. Anyway, the presence of the ghost the locals affectionately called the "mother-in-law" felt benign to me. After all, it was her house first. While she often played mischief on the guests at the restaurant, I had never seen anything ghostly figure-wise with my own physical eyes. I thought it was sort of fun sensing a presence on the physical plane, but I never physically heard anything or saw her with my own eyes, so I just went about my job. We would share stories with the clientele at the restaurant, and honestly that ghost was good for business. It wasn't until I worked in a different shop, also in the historic district of my hometown, that I had my first face-to-face ghostly encounter one winter's night.

It was in December, and the stores in the district always stayed open later for holiday shopping. That night the store had been crazy busy, I had worked alone, and I was anxious to total out, do the paperwork, and go home. As the last customer finally strolled out of the store a full fifteen minutes past closing time, I hurried to lock the front door. I went directly to the checkout counter and began totaling out the cash register. While the reports cycled through, I went to start the laborious job of turning off all the lights in the old house–turned–retail store.

This store was packed with displays, and because of the age of the building there were power strips everywhere with many items plugged into each of the strips. I started with the main overhead lights for the sales floor and then walked to the back of the shop. I sang along to the holiday songs playing on the radio and started flipping the power strips to the off position.

One by one, I made my way up toward the front of the store. Some of the power strips were easy to reach, while others you had to be a contortionist to get to. You literally had to get down on your hands and knees and crawl back through displays to get to them. The last strip to turn off was closest to the register area, way under a table and chairs. So I hunkered down, crawled under the table, and stretched way out to turn off that power strip.

"Gotcha!" I said in triumph. I eased out from under the table and stood back up. As I turned to go back to the register, a woman stood about three feet in front of me, smiling. She had dark hair pulled up on top of her head in a soft bun, and she was wearing a long charcoal-gray coat. I noticed stylish pointy-toed boots showing from under the hem of the pretty coat. She tipped her head to the side as if she were waiting for me, made eye contact, and smiled at me. I jolted and swore to myself, pressing my hands to my chest, as she had startled me. She only folded her hands at her waist, smiled again, and silently waited.

I closed my eyes in embarrassment and laughed. *Oh, no!* I thought. *I had locked a customer in the store with me and did not even know it!* I took a deep breath and turned to the woman with an apology on the tip of my tongue. I was sure to get in big trouble with my boss for this, and as I opened my eyes to begin my apology, she disappeared.

I watched her just *poof*—as in not be there any longer.

Then the room got icy cold. I stood there speechless for a second. That was not a physical person, as I had assumed. I stood there shaking with wonder. A ghost. A real ghost. Then I turned and slapped the main overhead lights back on and ran for the phone to call my husband. I told him what had happened and asked him to stay on the phone with me until I had to leave the store. While I wasn't afraid, it definitely made me a little jumpy. It was a hell of an experience, and while I have seen some crazy things in my life, felt cold spots, and witnessed things move in other haunted places, I had never actually seen a ghost standing right in front of me. *Wow.*

Later I did some digging on the history of the location of the building that I was working in and uncovered some startling facts about the place. I gathered my information at the local historical society. Ends up that the shop I worked in was a historical building that had been expanded in the 1980s. They had to dig into a steep hillside directly behind the house, and when they did, they uncovered bodies—lots of bodies. *Oops*. The construction crew discovered that they had accidentally dug into an old cemetery from the late 1700s.

Now, supposedly all of the inhabitants of the cemetery had been moved a century before to a newer, bigger Catholic cemetery a few blocks west and farther inland, away from the river. In actuality, it seems only the headstones of the very wealthy had been moved. According to local legend, Irish immigrants were paid twenty-five cents for every headstone that they moved to the new cemetery. Obviously not all of those graves had markers, and a couple hundred years later, in the 1980s, those disturbed graves were hastily covered back up with dirt. After the building's expansion was finished, they just sealed in that hill with some more dirt, covered that with asphalt, and called it good. Makes you cringe a little bit, doesn't it? And boy did that explain everything. Talk about Ghosts 101. A grave that has been disturbed or forgotten is a classic reason for a haunting.

I never saw the ghost lady again, but I sometimes felt a presence when I was in the store alone. I do have a theory as to why she manifested that night. All of the energy, activity, and good mood of the holiday shoppers probably added some "juice" to the atmosphere that she could use to manifest with. Also, there are always characters in costumes roaming the local historic district during the holiday festivities. People come from all over to see the Santas from around the world and Dickens's characters. You know, *A Christmas Carol*? As in characters dressed in Victorian-era clothing? When I first saw her, it never occurred to me to be surprised by her outfit. The long coat, puffy sleeves, pointy laced-up boots, even the hairstyle—I thought she was getting into the spirit of the holiday. I suppose, in a way, she was.

That was over eleven years ago, and it really left an impression on me. I imagine I saw her through my clairvoyance and also because she wanted to be seen. She probably figured out that by showing herself to me, I would accept what I saw and, more importantly, that I would try to figure out why she was there. So by sharing the information with the shopkeeper (who was less than amused) and the other folks at the historical society (who were absolutely thrilled), the kind, smiling lady ghost was not ignored; instead, she became a part of the local oral history of the building.

Today the area behind the shop is marked as a historic site of its own. Recently a replica of the original church was reconstructed and a marker erected for the burial site. Now it is noted that where the two corner buildings stand currently was originally the site of the town's earliest Catholic cemetery. A recent chat with the building's current shop employees has confirmed that all paranormal activity has ceased. Any psi-sensitive would still feel the presence of so many bodies buried close by, but the manifestation of the lady seems to have stopped. I don't think it's a coincidence that now that the graves of all of those unnamed people are remembered and noted, the manifestations have stopped. After all, no one wants to be forgotten.

Ouija Boards & Séances

The topic of Ouija boards is hotly debated among psychics and other folks in the paranormal field. Some people scoff at them and insist using one is only a silly game. Other psychically sensitive folks lovingly embrace spirit boards and work with them as a tool for contacting spirits, and others cringe from Ouija boards as if they were radioactive. Keep in mind that a consecrated spirit board that is ritually used, carefully maintained, and tended to is one thing; deciding to try a Ouija board just for the hell of it is another.

Whether you love or hate them, know this: Ouija boards are to be used with respect. They can be dangerous if you do not understand that this device has but one purpose, which is to allow communication between you and the ghosts or entities that are right here on our physical plane. In other words, it's a séance in a box.

A séance is defined as a gathering of people for the purpose of attempting communication with the spirits, which is exactly what you are doing when you work with a Ouija board. Now, if we look at this from a neutral point of view, the Ouija board is simple but effective tool for a séance as it can allow you to ask a spirit, ghost, or entity that is on the earthly plane a specific question, and in turn you can receive a specific answer. When you use a Ouija board, the answers are literally spelled out for you. Where things get a little shady is that spirits have been known to lie.

Some individuals would be shocked to know that the Ouija board is an actual tool—as in its sole purpose is to contact ghosts and spirits or entities, which, again, is correctly identified as a séance. But you don't contact the presence of your beloved grandmother who is at peace on the other side with a Ouija board. Try a medium for that, and see if Grandma is up for a little chat.

Remember, a medium acts as a bridge from our realm to the other side, while the Ouija board is all about communicating with spirits or energies that happen to be hanging around on this side. When you work with a Ouija board, there is no way to know who you are opening a door to. You don't get the opportunity to be selective. Whatever entity or spirit is the strongest comes through.

Look at it this way: Are all the people you meet lovely, friendly, and kind individuals whom you would be delighted to talk to? Absolutely not. Living people can be mean, rude, violent, or threatening, and the same can be said for spirits. If they are trapped on this plane, then it's probably for a reason, unfortunately. The use of a Ouija board can be a frightening experience for many people because it has been known to attract what I have seen described as lower-level entities. These nasty spirits feed on the fear of the people holding onto the planchette. Consider that fact carefully before you open up a portal to the spirits that you have no clue how to actually close.

Over the years, the most disturbing hauntings or spirit activity I have ever had the misfortune to check into all had their origins in the misuse of a Ouija board: from a bored middle-age housewife who thought it was a joke to a group of college students who used one in their rental home in the very spot where a young man had committed suicide a few years prior. They decided it would be fun to try communicating with him, just to see what would happen. Take a wild guess at what happened—nothing like having a half-dozen terrified young people descend on you during a book signing to beg for your help.

Once they calmed down enough to tell me what had happened, I figured out that they were playing with a Ouija board. I blistered their ears with a rather harsh lecture on the dangers of playing with a Ouija board. Again, it's a tool, not a toy. I gave them grief for running like hell when they got exactly what they asked for. I then reminded them that they called that former occupant of the home in and just left him there instead of staying put, sending him back, and cleaning up their own mess.

There are steps that can be taken to close down a portal that was opened by the careless use of a Ouija board. For more information on this, and for detailed information on how to cleanse a house from negative energies, please refer to my book *Practical Protection Magick*.

SLIders

Finally, we have another popular psychic phenomena to take a look at: SLIders. SLIder stands for Street Lamp Interference. SLI is a type of psychic phenomena that falls under the psychic experience category. If you want to get technical, the acronym SLIder's full meaning is Street Lamp Interference Data Exchange Receivers. In 1993 Hilary Evans compiled a collection of anecdotes on this phenomenon. The term stuck, and today people toss this acronym around often, but everyone wonders what it is exactly. To be clear: this is not an ability. This is a type of psychic phenomena that is randomly experienced.

SLI experiences typically involve the unexplained malfunction of electronic devices or the blowing out of light bulbs and street lamps around a specific individual on a regular basis. Since the SLI phenomena is typically anecdotal, it is often considered by academia to be meaningless, as it shows no practical purpose.

To that, I say…actually, I won't write down what I would say. It's a little rude. While there is no purpose to it, there are still plenty of annoying experiences that go along with this psychic phenomena anyway. Obviously those "academics" have never experienced the thrill of capping off a rotten day at work by coming home, turning on the light switch, and watching all of the overhead lights in the kitchen blow out with snaps and pops at the same time.

For anyone else who has experienced this phenomena, say it with me: *Yes, we have had the wiring checked. It's not the wiring.* This type of phenomena happens too often to be a coincidence (light bulbs blowing, batteries draining, and computers crashing) when psychics are upset, no matter where they happen to be. I will say that questions about this phenomena come up every time I lecture on psychic development. While the SLI phenomena is common, it still startles people and makes them a bit nervous.

If this is something you often experience, then instead of being anxious about it, just accept it as an occasional part, albeit an *annoying* occasional part, of the psychic package. The only caveat I have here is to suggest that you stock up on light bulbs and buy insurance for your cell phones and extended service plans for your electronics. Just a helpful tip to save you money when the inevitable problems with your electronics begin. Nope, not kidding. Even the special never-burn-out-for-years light bulbs don't last very long around SLIders.

If you are wondering whether this "talent" runs in families, the answer is yes. All of my adult children have the same type of SLI experiences. Piss them off or stress them out and watch their electronics, the light bulbs in their houses, or the computer systems, copiers, etc., at their jobs all go crazy. If you live with a SLIder, then stock up on extra light bulbs and learn to laugh. In fact, my husband has physically blocked me from turning on light switches when I am really upset. (Clever man. We've been married for over thirty years, and he knows me all too well.) As I researched this book, he was particularly delighted to discover this phenomenon actually has a name. He had always referred to it as "that annoying light bulb/computer thing you and the kids do."

It is important to remember that SLI phenomena is spontaneous and random, which is what makes it so hard to categorize, define, and prove. However, before you get discouraged, try looking at this topic from a different perspective. As previously discussed, heightened emotions cause all psychic experiences and abilities to come roaring out. Science and common sense would point out that your body and the impulses in your brain are electric, so when they spike or raise there is bound to be some interference. The most likely "target" to be affected would be the electronic devices closest to your person. Intense stress is bad for you. It can affect your health, too, not just your electronics. Now relax about this type of psychic phenomena before you blow up something else.

Some of the more common effects of the SLI phenomena include:

- street lamps flicker or go out whenever you are nearby (Street Lamp Interference)

- light bulbs blow out when you turn them off or on, especially when you are stressed/upset

- volume levels change on the TV, radio, or iPod for no apparent reason

- watches break, stop, or won't work properly when you wear them

- electronic toys act up, turning off and on seemingly by themselves

- the magnetic strip on credit/debit cards becomes damaged over and over, no matter how careful you are or how often you replace the card

- computers tending to go on the fritz whenever you are in a bad mood or under a large amount of stress

- a whole computer system or cash register system crashing when you are using it at work while you are particularly angry about your job

- batteries that constantly drain in your cell phone, no matter how new the phone or often you replace the battery

- problems with cell phone reception during a heightened emotional state

- problems with static on a landline phone during heightened emotional states

If you have experienced three or more of these SLI effects, then congratulations! You have just figured out the problem. It's just a bit of psychic phenomenon that you are experiencing. Oh sure, somebody somewhere is probably a little upset with me that I am not being more serious and intense about this topic. (Just call me psychic.) But seriously? If you experience SLIder phenomena, then you need to laugh and release some stress anyway; that is why it's happening in the first place. All that psychic energy, frustration, intensity, and, yes, stress is building up and looking for a handy electronic target.

Learn to face your problems and deal with your stress in a healthy way to relieve the pressure and lessen the severity of the SLIder experiences. What do you say we all learn to unclench, relax, lower our blood pressure, and let off some steam in a healthy way? I would suggest simple things such as taking a walk, working out, and of course meditation…so we can all find our inner Zen. Then, when we have all achieved inner peace, we can really go crazy and renew our warranties and protection plans on our computers and cell phones as a celebratory backup plan.

Chapter 7

Psychic Training

This chapter starts with an analogy. I'm going to share something with you, and let's see if you can sense how this applies to your own psychic development. A little over a year ago I joined a local gym and hired a personal trainer. I remember well that first day when I walked into that massive gym and saw all of those weights and various pieces of equipment. I was as intimidated as hell, and I do not intimidate easily. Looking around that gym, I literally broke into a nervous sweat. I was about to turn fifty and was struggling with the dreaded menopause weight gain. My blood pressure was too high, and all I could envision as I surveyed this foreign, chrome-filled landscape was a series of embarrassing workout mishaps because I would have no idea what I was doing. I am honestly one of the most uncoordinated women on the planet. I once took out half of a belly dance class with an silk veil; it was ugly.

I almost bolted out the gym doors, but then I told myself to cowboy up and ignored that sweat rolling down my back. I drew in a deep, steadying breath and took another, more careful look around that room. I realized there were all different sorts of folks in that gym working out. There was no one "type." Senior citizens, college-age students, and every age in between were cruising on treadmills and stationary bikes. Both men and women were using the free weights and equipment. Furthermore, the ages, body shapes, and abilities of the members were beautifully varied. Realizing there was no one stereotype of person in that gym—and that everyone was there to do their best—was comforting.

I did not leave that day. I stayed and signed up for a membership. I embraced the challenge to learn something new and enjoy the journey. Luckily for me, I was assigned a very nice young man for my training, and he and I got along very well. Has it been easy? Absolutely not. Turns out that sweet-faced, soft-voiced young man is diabolically inventive when it comes to training this smart-mouthed, middle-aged woman. Over the past year I have worked hard on strength training and increasing my overall physical fitness.

There were days I would limp home, whimper though a shower, collapse on the couch, and be shot for the rest of the day. Then, after a few months, I would come home, have a protein shake, hit the showers, and be energized for the rest of my day. These days I have learned to love the incredibly sore feeling that comes the day after a new or a hard workout. Every time I feel that, I am reminded that I just trained a new group of muscles. Also, I am reminded that my discomfort and awkwardness will fade, and in their place improved strength, skill, and endurance will be gained. Most importantly, I have had to relearn everything I thought I knew about myself and what I am actually capable of. Today I am at the start of another year on my journey of personal improvement, and I am more excited than ever.

So did you figure out the comparison of strength training to the personal training of psychic development? Yeah, I admit that was about as subtle as a brick to the forehead. However, think about the similarities of psychic development and strength training. It does not matter what age you are or what your previous level of experience is. When it comes to working on psychic development, everyone will have their own personal issues to overcome. We all have specific areas to target and personal psychic goals we want to work toward. Sure, you might feel awkward or intimidated when you start developing your own psychic abilities, but with a little assistance and guidance (in the form of this book), and plenty of hard work on your part, you will see improvement and an increase in your skills.

Bottom line: training is training. Whether you are learning to do deadlifts for the first time or trusting your own psychic experiences and expanding your own psychic abilities, you will get out of this journey whatever you are willing to put into it. Yes, psychic development absolutely takes time and work. To develop any new muscles, be they physical or psychic, takes effort, repetition, faith in yourself, and keeping your eye on the long-term goal. If you can do all that, you will succeed. Let me show you a few ways that you can start working out those mental muscles.

Work Those Psychic Muscles!

To begin your training and get those psychic abilities a good workout, let's start with some exercises and four days' worth of homework. I'll tell you now that these assignments may surprise you; however, there is a method to my madness. For the first three days I want you to experience a day devoted to an awareness of one of your physical senses. You will focus on seeing, hearing, and touching. Why are we starting with the physical senses? Because if you tune in to what your physical senses are telling you, it makes it easier to discern when a psychic sense is at work. Finally, on the fourth day I want you to be aware of what you experience or sense emotionally. This will be fun, and I bet you will be surprised at the insights you gain into yourself.

For this four-day homework, you will need a spiral notebook and a pencil or pen. Also, if you have a smartphone and you come up with something of importance that you don't want to forget, make a note with the apps on your phone. I do this often if I am out and about and a thought comes to me for a book I am working on. I hit the notes app, tap the microphone, and start talking, so my thought is saved as a note. Finally, you will need about a half-hour of your time at the end of the day to note down your sensory experiences for that particular day. A paragraph will do fine.

It is important to point out that you should go about your business. Work, play, family, kids…whatever you typically do in your regular routine. It is important to stick to your regular routine because, let's face it, psychic experiences do not arrange themselves neatly into your schedule. They simply pop up and then you have to learn to be able to deal with them and keep rolling with your life at the same time.

Day One: Seeing Day

Today I want you to really look at the world around you. Look at the environment around you as if you were seeing it for the first time. Think about how carefully you look around when you travel anywhere new. For example, when you go to a park for the first time, you would look carefully around and get the lay of the land. You would look for points of interest to explore. Most folks gather their impressions of places and people visually. See things how they physically are: colors, plants, trees, the landscape, the sky, the sun, the moon, the stars, people, pets, and animals in the wild. Go to a garden or visit a greenhouse or go to the art museum. Now look carefully around. What do you see? What colors, shapes, and patterns capture your attention? Don't overthink your visual impressions; just look. Then, at the end of the day, write down what you were aware of on a visual level.

Day Two: Hearing Day

For day two you will have to listen closely. Today I want you to really listen to the world around you. Today is the day to keep your ears open and to listen to what your environment really sounds like. This might be a tough assignment for some because this means no music in the background. Seriously—how much sound do you drown out? If you listen to the radio in the car or wear headphones/earbuds and block out noise with your iPod on the way to work, how much are you *really* aware of the sounds occurring around you?

I'd like you to listen to your environment as if you were hearing it for the first time. Think about how you stop and are silent, listening, when you are out and alone in nature. Today you need to get yourself out and in nature however you can. Head to the nearest park, woods, mountains, prairie, desert, or beach, stand in silence, and listen. Are your surroundings silent? I doubt it. There is sound everywhere. Listen for the sound of water—the river that rolls by, the surf that crashes, the stream that babbles. Listen to the melody of the wind. There is the breeze ruffling through the leaves of the trees. Are you noticing the different calls of birds, animals, and insects? Focus on the sounds you hear and note what impressions you gather from the physical sense of hearing. Then, at the end of the day, write down what you were aware of on an auditory level.

Day Three: Touching Day

Today I want you to reach out and touch the world around you. Use your hands and feel the shapes and textures of your environment around you as if you were noticing it for the first time. Take a moment and pass your fingers over your face and over your own skin. Run your hands through your hair and down your arms. Place your hands over your chest and feel the strength of your beating heart. During the course of your day, make a point of touching as many different kinds of objects as possible. A fun idea to explore this sense is to go to the produce section of a grocery store. If you could only choose your produce by touch, what sort would you choose? (Be polite and purchase something while you are in the grocery store; don't just feel up the produce!) Have a seat in the grass in your yard and run your hands through the grass and clover. Touch the flowers in your garden, jump in a leaf pile, or sink your hands in the snow and see what information you gather with your physical sense of touch.

Another suggestion is to give your pets a good brushing and make them happy. Spend some time scratching your dog's ears or rubbing your cat's chin. Touch is powerful; how did it affect your pets? What information did you gather by your sense of touch today? Then, at the end of the day, write down the different sensations you experienced through your physical touch.

Day Four: Sensing Day

Today I want you to stop and sense the world around you. Ask yourself how your environment physically makes you feel—are you comfortable or uncomfortable? Calm, indifferent, or anxious? Experience your environment as if you were sensing it for the first time. How do certain people and places make you feel? Are you happy, angry, inspired, or energized? A good way to stretch your emotional sensing outside the box is to go hug a tree. Seriously. Go find a big old tree and wrap your arms around the trunk. Place your cheek carefully against the bark and close your eyes. (By closing your eyes, you force your other senses to come out and play.) Now take a deep breath in and relax; what do you sense from that old tree?

Another suggestion is to spend some time with the young children in your life. What do you notice about the atmosphere in the room when a child is laughing in delight or crying in frustration? How do the regular experiences of your daily life make you feel? Don't overthink your emotional impressions, just experience them. Then, at the end of the day, write down what you were aware of or what you became aware of on an emotional level.

Sensory Homework Notes

Before you read this next part, I would like you to be sure to actually do the four-day sensory homework. Otherwise what you are about to read will influence any results and information that you receive, so no peeking…oh, and I'll know if you do. (Trust me: I'm psychic.) If you want to develop your psychic abilities, then do the work first and *then* read why I insisted that you do. So no whining—get to work!

When I wrote this chapter, I sent this sensory homework to a couple of my friends and had them do the assignments. Their notes on their homework were very interesting. These two people had never met before; one lives in Los Angeles, California, while the other is in rural southern Missouri. One was more claircognizant/intuitive and was married with kids, and the other friend was clairsentient/empathic and single. While they each led very different lifestyles, they both were open to learning more about their own psychic abilities, and their homework notes had many similarities. Both of my friends enjoyed the first three daily assignments, and their responses were pretty much what I had expected. But it was their comments on the fourth day that confirmed my theory and proved the point of this entire exercise.

By the fourth day (the sensing/feeling day), their dominant psychic ability had kicked in strongly. That was the day I told them to focus only on their emotions and what they felt and sensed around them, and after three days of focusing only on information gathered by their physical senses, their dominant psychic abilities were raring and ready to go. I suspected that this would be the case but did not want to show my hand, so to speak, so I kept quiet and waited. They did not disappoint me.

One of my friends noted that as soon as she opened her eyes on the fourth day, she knew something was wrong—and thus her day began with a premonition. She put her premonition to work. (Refer to chapter 1 for information on that, should you need a refresher.) Narrowing down where she was going to experience the challenges for her day, she then psyched herself up. Those challenges ended up ranging from minor annoyances with her children's daycare to administrative snafus and dramas at her job. However, because she had that heads up from her intuition, she was prepared. She was more than able to handle the challenges of her day one crisis at a time. Her heightened awareness allowed her to tap into her claircognizance/psychic intuition as well as her clairsentience/psychic empathy during the day. That way she "just knew" when the trouble was about to surface, and this helped her to navigate a very trying day.

At the end of the fourth day, she fell asleep with the hunch that the next day would be better. Sure enough, the next morning she got some very positive feedback from an editor over an article she had been fretting over. She also came to the realization that she had, in fact, been combining her psychic abilities of clairsentience/psychic empathy successfully with her claircognizance/intuition. By working with these two abilities at the same time and riding the wave, so to speak, any psychic information she was gleaning during the day was clearer and quicker for her to interpret correctly.

My second friend, who has impressive psychic empathy abilities, really enjoyed the sensory homework. She has always described herself as "painfully empathic" and approached the homework as a personal challenge. On day one she was delighted with her visual impressions of the minute details of things, right down to the energetic emanations she could see coming from various items themselves. On her second day she discovered that she was tuning in to sounds on a level she had never noticed before. Sounds at a distance were clearer, and music she danced to during an exercise class seemed richer. By day three she was excited to rediscover just how much knowledge she could gain from her own two hands and sense of touch, from the texture of a yoga mat and the strength in her own physical body to the silkiness of her own hair as she brushed it out after her workout. She reported that by focusing on the tangible information she gathered through the act of touch, day three's assignment had given her a new way to communicate and honor her physical self.

On her fourth day she stated that after three days of wholeheartedly embracing her physical impressions, she had realized something very important: her habit of tiptoeing around the fullness of her physical senses did not serve her as well as embracing them did. She explained that what she learned from the homework was that surrendering to her clairsentience/psychic empathy was much more healthy than cringing away from it. She also realized that when she worked from a place of less resistance, she received more useful and clearer information from the psychic realm.

Hey, Wait! That's Not What Happened to Me on Day Four!

Now before someone panics and starts jumping up and down, saying that they did not get a barrage of psychic illumination on day four, just relax. What did you discover on day four? What did focusing on your emotions and how you react to situations teach you about yourself? Go ahead and check the notes you made for day four's homework. There are no wrong or right answers here, as this assignment was all about you: what you learned, what you felt, and what you experienced. Study your comments on day four's homework closely. This way you will have a clearer idea on what pushes your buttons emotionally. Understanding how your own emotions work and how you react to different people and situations will allow for an easier time when it comes to distinguishing between a premonition or simple stress and mild anxiety.

Also remember, as was discussed in the first chapter, that times of intense emotions do tend to bring psychic experiences out and to the forefront. So once again, understanding the difference between your typical emotional responses and an intense psychic gut response or the stop-you-in-your-tracks emotions of a premonition is important. The only way you are going to know is to pay attention and validate the experiences.

These exercises were all about expanding your awareness. What have you learned about your perceptions? What did you learn when you shifted your awareness to a new level? If you're not sure, go back and read your homework. There is your answer. That's what the homework's notes were for. Validation is a beautiful thing.

Simple Training for the Five Cs: Claircognizance, Clairaudience, Clairvoyance, Clairsentience & Clairtangence

Here is a psychic training exercise for you. It will also help you very quickly to confirm just where your talents lie. Remember that many people are a mixture of psychic abilities. The following exercise is one that I taught my own kids when they were young, and it's one I currently have my teenage niece working on so she can flex those psychic muscles a bit.

What you need for this is a deck of ordinary playing cards. Find the ace of spades, the ace of hearts, and the ace of diamonds; pull those three cards from the deck. Set the rest of the deck aside. We use the ace of spades because often that is a bold graphic and you want to picture that black ace so you can find it using your own psychic ability. We use the two other red aces so you can focus on the black ace and not get confused by concentrating on other numbers. This is all about color and symbols.

On a flat surface (try the kitchen table or counter), place the three ace cards facedown. Now mix them all up so you have no idea which card is which, then arrange them (still facedown) in a horizontal line. Now hold your hand out over the cards one at a time and try to find the black ace of spades. Choose the card you think is the ace of spades and see if you are correct. Repeat for a total of ten times. Note how many times you were correct.

Now to take this deceptively simple exercise to the next level. Looking over your past results, ask yourself how you chose the ace of spades when you were correct. Did you "just know"? That's claircognizance, or intuition. Maybe you saw the correct card in your mind's eye? That's clairvoyance. Did your inner voice tell you which one it was? That would be clairaudience. Or did you just feel it? Perhaps you got an emotional response on the correct card? Then that is clairsentience, or psychic empathy. Lastly, did you try physically touching the cards to divine the correct card? And if you touched them, then were you more accurate? Or did touching the cards give you an insight, feeling, or vision? If you were able to discern the correct card by touch, then that is clairtangency, or psychic touch. If touching the cards gave you an insight or a vision or you were able to hear your inner voice more clearly and correctly, then you have combined clairtangency with another psychic ability.

The first time I showed my niece this exercise was on Christmas Day at my mother's house. She had come to me quietly and asked me to help her understand her precognitive dreams. I realized that her abilities were beginning to kick in and were overwhelming her, as is often the case in teenagers. So while the rest of the family played billiards, we used a hassock for a table and sat on the floor practicing this card exercise. Within a few moments she was getting frustrated, especially as I was able to find that ace of spades almost every time. She said she didn't think she would ever get the hang of it. I encouraged her to try it again. I shuffled and rearranged the cards, and told her that this time she should try touching the cards to see if that helped. I also encouraged her to relax.

While she and I were talking, my adult son, Kyle, was walking around the pool table, looking for a good angle for his next shot. As he walked past the two of us, he stopped, backed up, reached over his cousin's shoulder, and quickly turned over the ace of spades, first try. He winked at her, and my niece started to laugh. Kyle encouraged her to try again and told her not to think about it so hard—just go for it. My niece shuffled the cards, took a deep breath, and then laughed, a little embarrassed because now all three of my adult children were standing there, all gathered around, watching her and giving encouragement. This time she touched each facedown card, one after another, at the edges. Then she took a deep breath and turned over the ace of spades. The look on her face was priceless.

I recently did this find-the-ace-of-spades exercise at a conference I attended. I explained how easy this process was and showed the three cards to the couple hundred people who were gathered in the lecture hall. I put the cards facedown on the table and mixed them all up so I would have no idea where the ace of spades was. As I explained how the psychic exercise was to be performed, I reached down in midsentence and lifted a card into the air. It was the ace of spades. Knowing full well some of the folks in the room thought it was a card trick, I asked for a volunteer to come to the front of the room to try this out for themselves.

Not surprisingly, no one volunteered. Most people don't like being put on the spot, so I chose someone at random. As the first person approached me, he announced that he considered himself to be more intuitive. I suggested that he shuffle the cards and see how that worked: boom. First try. He waved the card excitedly to the crowd and got a round of applause. Now I had lots of volunteers.

The second time I chose a boy of about twelve who had been sitting with his parents. I invited him up, took him through the steps, and watched him balk. Clearly he was second-guessing himself. He was crushed when he didn't pull the ace of spades. So, as I had done with my niece, I made him slow down and touch each card first. I made him laugh and relax, which I'm sure was not easy for a boy in front of a couple hundred people. But sure enough, as he touched each card, I watched his shoulders drop and he began to unwind a bit. Then he correctly flipped over the ace of spades with a excited shout.

He asked me if he could try it once more, so I mixed up the cards well and stood back. He took his time and thoughtfully touched each facedown card, then correctly turned over that ace of spades again. While he smiled at the applause he received, I asked him how he discerned which card was the black ace. He answered simply, "Once I touched them, I felt where it was." So I told him and the group in the room that this meant he was using clairtangency with clairsentience. After the lecture concluded, there was a rush up to the table where folks stood in line to try it out for themselves.

This find-the-ace-of-spades game is a great way to practice and discover just which psychic abilities you are bringing to the table. It can be
done with friends or by yourself. It is an appropriate psychic exercise for
anyone aged teen to adult. Most of all, just have fun with this. If you relax,
you will get better results. Get in there and work it! A little hands-on psychic exercise is just the ticket. I bet you will surprise yourself with the
results.

Honing Your Skills, Accepting Your Talents

At this point in the book, you should have a pretty good idea of what sort
of psychic ability or abilities you are working with. Oh, I imagine somebody is disappointed because I did not put a "what flavor of psychic are
you" quiz in this book. However, I did not do that for a couple of very
good reasons. Number one: it's been done to death. Number two: I honestly detest quizzes, for the simple fact that rarely are folks honest with
their answers. Most folks are intuitive enough to know they can choose
their quiz answers in a way that will slant the outcome of any personality
quiz. (Recall that everyone has psychic abilities; it is simply up to them as
to whether they choose to develop them and work with them.) Because of
people's natural intuition, when it comes to quizzes they answer as they
wish they were or as they think they should instead of how they really
think and feel.

So instead of wasting time with a quiz, let me ask you this: What have
you learned about yourself so far? Don't panic. Just answer the question
honestly and right now. What does your heart or gut tell you? When you
consider it, what looks or sounds right to you? When you were reading
earlier in the book about the various psychic experiences and abilities,
which ones made you have an aha moment? Announce the answer to the
question of what you have discovered about your own talents out loud
and do it right now. Embrace and accept what you have discovered about
yourself.

Once you have recognized and embraced the psychic talents you posses, that means you are ready to move forward. Now the challenge begins. You hone your skills by working with them every day and as often as you can. Practice does indeed make perfect. So get to work and see how far you can take your psychic skills! To hone your abilities, you need to practice and keep your physical senses sharp; that way, your psychic skills are accessible to you whenever you need them. That being said, here is a psychic development secret: the best way to hone your skills is to keep track of them.

As was suggested in the introduction, keep a journal and note how your experiences and own unique psi-abilities play out. That validation from your notekeeping then brings confidence. It is not for me to tell you what type of psychic talents you possess. It is for me to teach you about psychic experiences and abilities, allowing you the freedom to discover the truth about yourself and your personal psychic powers on your own. Good teachers do not do the work for the students; instead, they present the information, guide and encourage, and then stand back as the students embrace the information, gain the knowledge, and then stand strong on their own.

Well, look at you, standing there all strong and confident!

I had a hunch you would be.

EVERYTHING IS FUNNY *as long as*
it is happening to somebody else.

Will Rogers

Chapter 8

Psychic First Aid, Protection, and Self-Defense

As I moved to the final chapters of this book, a little synchronicity decided to have fun with me. It was mid-January, and earlier in the month I had endured a week-long bout with the flu. I was just starting to feel better and was trying desperately to get back to my regular workout routine at the gym and get back on track with this book. My publicist had scheduled me for two separate appearances on radio shows. Seems there was a run on radio shows wanting to talk to a psychic. I'm guessing it was a what's-in-store-for-the-new-year sort of deal.

The first gig was only supposed to last a half-hour; however, the interviewer had a good sense of humor and was so impressed by my over-the-phone psychic and tarot readings for the folks who called in that I ended up doing two hours live on air. It was a lot of fun, but it also was tiring. The second radio interview a few days later was only twenty minutes long. In the pre-interview the announcer was somewhat passive-aggressive. He informed me that he did not really believe in psychics but kept insisting that he was open-minded. Oh joy.

So with the second radio interview I worked hard to be polite and cheerful, and of course I used a lot of humor, which is my default mode when I am aggravated but can't afford to show it. The second interview was blessedly brief, and as we finished up the interview, I explained to the announcer how it was possible to do long-distance readings over the phone. I said that for me it was sort of like remote viewing, as in I pictured in my mind where the person was I was reading for (in this case, the city and state they were in while I was speaking to them on the phone), then I honed in on their voice and read them. Then, without him asking me to, I read the announcer on air. I had picked up some psychic information while he had been speaking, and let's just say he believes in psychics now.

I chuckled a bit after the radio interview was finished, and my friends who had been listening across the country via online access blew up my cell phone with the way the interview had turned out. My publicist was delighted, and I was feeling happy, a wee bit smug, and also little lightheaded. I went to bed early that night and planned to hit the gym first thing in the morning. And you know what they say about the best-laid plans...

I woke up the next morning with a psychic hangover the size of Montana. A psychic hangover feels remarkably similar to a hangover that comes from drinking a little too much, only without the alcohol—as in you have no energy and you feel out of sorts and mentally fuzzy. While a psychic hangover is energetic in nature, it can include physical symptoms. Depending on the severity, you can be gifted with a dull headache, nausea, and body aches. This physical reaction to overdoing psychic work is also called an energetic overextension.

Technically an overextension happens when an individual goes beyond their capabilities psychically or physically. It's not unlike doing dead lifts at the gym: if you lift too heavy too quickly, you'll feel it right away. Because of that overextension of your lifting ability, it might take a few days for your muscles to stop screaming at you. But you will heal, and then you can slowly but surely *and* safely add to the amount of weight you are lifting. This way, you can slowly build up your strength and correctly learn to lift heavier amounts successfully in the future. The same analogy can be applied to flexing your psychic strength. If you go overboard, you become overextended. Bottom line: an energetic overextension, or psychic hangover, sucks.

The morning after the second radio interview, I staggered out of bed, took something for my walloping headache, and forced myself to eat a good high-protein breakfast. I made myself a cup of strong tea and prayed for the caffeine to kick in, then I settled in at my desk in my home office to work, which was a less than pleasant prospect. At one point I put my head in my hands and admitted that I felt like an energetic truck had run me over. Hello, overextension. I didn't feel so smug now. I got through my day and told myself that I would go to the gym later that afternoon.

My husband took one look at me that afternoon while I stood folding laundry and told me to go sit on the couch. I ignored that advice and kept at it. As I went to put the laundry away, I literally walked into the door frame. He looked at me and said quietly, "I listened to your radio interview while I was at work last night."

"What did you think?" I grimaced at him while I rubbed my shoulder. Maybe I'll be graceful in my next life.

He walked over, took the folded laundry away from me, and quietly said, "You were accurate as hell, babe. But when you do a long-distance reading like that, it costs you physically, doesn't it?"

"Yes, it does. Because I drop my shields and reach out energetically over long distances," I admitted.

He gave me a stern look. Then he took my arm, steered me to the couch, and told me to relax for a while. I am not the meek and mild type of personality, but I kept my mouth shut and stayed on the couch for a couple hours because damn it, he was right. So I slowed down my routine for a couple of days and recouped, as energy spent has to be regained.

I have probably just blown my image by admitting that I have limits. I am not a superhero. It's a bird, it's a plane…it's Super Psychic! Not. If I overextend, then I need to recoup spent psychic energy just like everybody else. This isn't a comic book or the movies. In real life, if you overdo the use of your psychic abilities, you will have to apply some psychic first aid and then rebuild on an energetic level.

Now before someone begins to wonder if every time they use their psychic abilities they will be staggering around and bouncing off door frames the following day, let me clarify a few things here. First off, I had just gotten over the flu. I had completed a hard workout at the gym that day, ran several errands afterwards, and had been writing for hours…and that was before I found out about the radio interview. Secondly, I ended up doing an unplanned medium-style reading—also long-distance, over the phone—a few hours before the radio interview. I had pushed myself hard that day both physically and psychic ability–wise, and then again during the radio interview that evening.

I should know better than to try reading someone remotely when I was already tired; however, I got caught up in the moment while I was on air. I was annoyed at the radio announcer's condescending attitude and what I am sure he thought were his clever innuendos. Because I was tired before the interview began, I wasn't as cautious as I normally would be. I let my emotions dictate my behavior. Sure, it made for a great interview, and I impressed the hell out of a skeptic, but I still had to deal with the physical cost of spending energy when I was already worn down. In other words, I overextended—and then the next day I paid the energetic price.

How to Deal with Psychic Hangovers and Overextensions: Recharge and Recoup

I find that one of the bigger concerns people have about their own psychic development is, "What if I overextend my psychic abilities too much and it wears me down?" Well, honestly, kids, it's going to. There: I said it, and look—the world did not end.

Don't drop this book in horror and cringe away from the topic. Stay calm and think this through logically. If you strain your muscles doing something more physically demanding, then you are bound to be a bit tired and have some sore muscles the next day. Psychic development is no different because you are simply working out new mental muscles. When it comes to psychic development and experimenting with your psychic abilities, you have basically given yourself both a mental and a psychic workout. You may not experience a psychic hangover; however, if you overextend yourself, you may feel a bit more emotional than normal or simply worn down. How do you fix that? It's nothing a little R&R—or recoup and recharge—won't cure.

So, my advice? Go apply a little psychic first aid and start recharging and recouping. It's a four-step process that is simple, fun, and good for you.

Four Steps of Psychic First Aid

Step One: Take a Break and Take a Nap

Like the batteries in your cell phone, notebook, or laptop, if you drain the energy down to a low level, those devices do need to recharge. Turn off your brain for an hour. Get comfy on the couch, shut your eyes, perhaps listen to some soothing music or relaxing sounds of nature from a white noise track, and have a snooze. Do not gab on the phone or run around; just give yourself an hour or so to recharge your own energetic batteries.

Step Two: Have a Gentle Workout

Seriously, don't even whine at me and tell me how tired you are. Nope. Let's go! Now is the time to get up and move. Go to the gym and break a little sweat. This will help to release any psychic toxins you may have picked up. Don't go crazy and overdo it—just have a nice workout and get your endorphins flowing. Those "feel good" hormones will do the trick to helping you feel better quickly. The natural lift exercise gives you is the best way to combat any psychic hangover.

Alternately, if you do not have a gym membership, you could do yoga, tai chi, or a workout DVD at home. Take a thirty-minute walk around the neighborhood or local park or do a few miles of easy jogging or biking—that ought to do it. Another suggestion is to work in your garden. Pull weeds, trim the flowers, or rake some leaves. Are you a dancer? Well, then go bust a move, Zumba, belly dance, ballet, break out the tap shoes, ballroom dance…no matter how you choose to exercise, you should get your heart pumping and your body moving.

Step Three: Go Outside

If your step two involved being outdoors, good for you! If you were inside and exercising for step one, then proceed to going outdoors for a time. Either way, while you are out there in nature, soak up some of the sun's healing energy and allow the breeze to blow any residual energy off and away from yourself. Letting the elements of nature remove any residual energy is a simple fix to feeling overwhelmed by other people's memories.

Residual psychic energy from other folks feels sort of like light spider webs—you know, the kind you can feel but never see? So when I get that feeling after readings, I take my happy self on a nice long two-mile walk and let those endorphins and the power of nature do its work burning off and blowing away any residual threads of energy. Try it! Get some exercise. It works out very well. When the workout is over and the endorphins are flowing, you will have a natural pick-me-up.

Step Four: Pamper Yourself Just a Bit

Indulge in a nice warm bath or shower after your workout and time outside. Visualize all the fatigue rinsing off your body and flowing harmlessly down the drain. Eat a healthy meal with plenty of protein. If you notice that your blood sugar levels are crashing, then you need protein (just like it was discussed in chapter 5's survival guide). Also, you can try a low-sugar sports drink (after the protein) to replenish your fluids and electrolytes. Be sure to drink lots of water, which flushes your system and keeps you hydrated.

Finally, it is important to stick with your regular routine as much as possible. When you have the opportunity, do something that makes you happy: go to the movies, read a fun book, scrapbook, paint, plant a new container full of flowers, or meet a friend for lunch. Take a little "me time." Allow your psychic abilities to recoup and recharge. Keep yourself distracted with happy things and top that off with a good night's sleep, and you will be as good as new in a couple of days.

Psychic Attacks and Psychic Protection

The topic of psychic attack often frightens people when they begin to study psychic development. Conversely, many individuals decide to study psychic development to learn ways to stop the effects of what they perceive to be negative energy from others. Psychic attack is common but rarely as dramatic as some folks would have you believe. Psychic attack comes in many forms, most often in everyday ways that may surprise you. For example, anybody who has ever had to face down an argumentative or condescending coworker, a jealous colleague, a nasty-tempered boss, a spiteful ex, an angry soon-to-be-former friend, or a disapproving relative has had to deal with a form of psychic attack.

Psychic attack: The unconscious or purposeful focusing of psychic or mental energies to bring emotional harm to another individual.

A psychic attack is, in essence, a personal attack. It scrapes away at your confidence and your ego until you feel worthless. It is similar to when you are confronted with the old "big me, little you" scenario. It can also be a situation where the attacker feels, for some reason, that they are going to be the one to take you down. There are many reasons for this, but typically the motivator is plain old jealousy. You have something they want, and they are angry or envious that you have what they don't have.

Energetic attacks like this happen all the time, typically by folks who have no idea what they are doing. You get hit with a big old dose of hatred; it may or may not be on purpose. However, if this has enough force behind it, the results will be the same. It's the aggressor's intent that fuels a psychic attack and can make it more powerful. Keep in mind that emotions fuel psychic abilities, and intense emotions like anger, envy, and hate turn up the volume on an attack. We can all be involuntarily affected by other people's negative thoughts and emotions.

However, it is important to remember that the majority of psychic attacks come from people who have no idea what they are actually doing. They just get angry or jealous, and then all that emotional energy gets directed at you. Since you are working on psychic development, you should expect that you are going to feel the effects of that negativity in one form or another. Think of this as another form of psychic training. Rise to the occasion and work your way through. Armed with knowledge and a plan of action, you can handle anything that gets thrown at you energetically, be it accidental or purposeful.

How do you know when you are on the receiving end of a psychic attack? Well, there are several physical symptoms or real-life manifestations that you should pay attention to. Your first clue will likely be a premonition that something is wrong, so pay attention to your premonitions. I recommend that you use the techniques from chapter 1's section on "Successfully Solving the Mysterious Premonition," and then calmly and thoughtfully look for answers. Furthermore, I would suggest that you change your premonition investigative questions to a more personal nature.

I would go with something along these lines: Is someone directing negative psychic energy at me? Do I know them? Who are they? Is this ego- or temper-motivated? See how your body reacts. Look for the "hit" that was described for you at the beginning of the book, and then narrow your search by a process of elimination.

If you are more intuitive/claircognizant, then expect that you will know that something is off. Check your gut hunches in regard to the situation. If you are clairaudient, check in and see what your inner voice has to say. Does anything sound off to you? This can manifest as an energy that sounds discordant to your psychic hearing.

If you are clairvoyant, take a moment, close your eyes, focus on your third eye area, and see what visions unfold. Also look around with your physical eyes. Does anything look wrong or seem out of place? An empath should ask themselves what they notice emotionally when they consider the possibility or the possible perpetrator. Someone with clairtangent abilities can try reading a photo of themselves or quietly run their hand on the front door of their home. (Why the front door? Well, that energy has to get in from somewhere; likely it's coming in the front door.) See what you discover by using psychic touch.

Some other symptoms to watch for are what I call the heebie-jeebies— you know this one: it's that feeling that something is either stuck on your clothes or a bug is crawling on you. Then you check, looking for dirt on your face or a smudge on your clean shirt, and start brushing at unseen lint or your clothes, only to discover that there is nothing actually there. You just get nervous, itchy, or twitchy for no apparent reason—that's a classic case of the heebie-jeebies.

Feeling that you are being watched is another classic indicator. Others include feeling drained of all of your personal energy; a heaviness in your neck, shoulders, or chest; an ache in the solar plexus; or vivid and recurring nightmares that are especially violent and disturbing. While these symptoms may seem ominous or frightening, they are not. These are big red "pay attention" flags that your own subconscious is waving in your face.

It is important to realize that these symptoms are your body and mind's way of getting your attention. Acknowledge what your body and subconscious are trying to tell you, take action with some active psychic self-defense, and you are well on your way to ending the problem. I also strongly suggest using a divinatory tool for a secondary confirmation of a possible psychic attack. I do prefer tarot cards for this, as they can give you a very detailed and dimensional answer. However, if you are proficient in runes, that would work just as well.

A Tarot Reading to Confirm an Energetic Attack

Here are the directions and layout for a reading to confirm an energetic attack. This is a straightforward four-card layout that will quickly show you what you need to know. Begin by shuffling the cards well. While you are doing so, say out loud, "Show me what I need to know: Am I under emotional or psychic attack?" Then deal four cards. Arrange the cards in a horizontal line going from left to right.

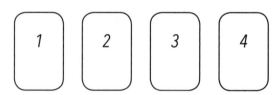

- Card 1 shows you if you are truly under attack.

- Card 2 displays clues about who is perpetrating the attack.

- Card 3 indicates the best way to neutralize
  the energy being sent.

- Card 4 points out what lessons there are
  to be learned from the situation.

Here are a few tips for this particular reading. Watch for major arcana cards. Major arcana cards in a spread add weight and importance to the reading. If there are two or more major arcana cards in this particular reading, then you will know that the situation is intense and needs your immediate response. Also, take careful consideration of any court cards that pop up in this reading because the court cards—the tarot deck's kings, queens, knights, and pages—show personalities and people. There is a general rule of thumb for identifying people in a tarot reading when it comes to court cards.

- the suit of cups symbolizes people with dark blond or pale blond hair and blue or green eyes

- the suit of wands represents people with fair complexions, blond or red hair, and pale blue or gray eyes

- the suit of swords illustrates people with brown hair and green, blue, or hazel eyes

- the suit of pentacles corresponds to people with dark hair, dark brown eyes, and deep complexions

Admittedly, not every hair color, eye color, and skin tone is represented here, so you should think of the suggestions above more as guidelines than actual rules. The court cards also have links to the twelve signs of the zodiac. For example, if the physical traits do not match up, then you should consider the personality traits associated with the court cards of the following suits. This can help you narrow down your search and figure out where the attacking energy is coming from.

Astrological Signs, Personality Traits, and Elements Associated with the Court Cards

Cups: Cancer, Scorpio, and Pisces; mystical, empathic, and emotional; water

Wands: Aries, Leo, and Sagittarius; clever, cerebral, and witty; fire

Swords: Gemini, Libra, and Aquarius; fiery, passionate, and outgoing; air

Pentacles: Taurus, Virgo, and Capricorn; earthy, practical, and easygoing; earth

Remember that tarot cards are used as a psychic springboard. Combine this secondary confirmation reading with your own psychic abilities. This will give you a better chance of identifying the problem while also getting more specific information on how to combat it using psychic self-defense.

Psychic Self-Defense

Psychic self-defense is the act of protecting or defending yourself from negative psychic energy, or the adverse/depressing thoughts of another. Practicing psychic self-defense can also keep you from being emotionally vulnerable to the barbs, digs, and mind games of everyday life. Think of psychic self-defense as a little extra insulation from the jealous, emotionally draining, or unhappy people we all encounter.

For effective psychic self-defense, the first thing you need is a deeper level of awareness. Become more aware of your surroundings on both energetic and physical levels. You will achieve this by using all of your psychic abilities and your physical senses. Refer to your homework from the psychic training chapter; think about how much more aware you were when you focused on an individual physical sense. By being tuned in this way and then combining that with your psychic abilities, you can easily keep track of what is going on energetically around you.

We have spent the last seven chapters working on the development and advancement of your psychic abilities. With that increased perception and ability also comes a new level of sensitivity to the negative emotions and energy of those around you. Increased psychic sensitivity is, in fact, a double-edged sword—as that "sword" you have been honing can cause problems or pain if you are not thoughtful with how you wield it. However, this psychic sensitivity that we have been cultivating has indeed become your finest weapon in the energetic defense of your person.

When it comes to the topic of psychic self-defense, you will read plenty of books on psychic development that give you the sweetness-and-light routine. There are sources out there that will loftily suggest your only recourse is to send universal love to an energetic attacker and all will be well, since as psychics we are all such evolved and enlightened beings, and therefore we should realize that there are sad, benighted individuals in the world who do not have the benefit of our vast experience and superior moral high ground. So sending universal love or healing energy to your psychic attacker is naturally your only option…

Well, let's all just hold hands and sing "Kumbaya."

Seriously? I have several issues with that train of thought, and here is why. First off, that type of psychic moral high ground strikes me as snooty—not to mention that the New Age mindset of "white light and universal love" can get you pretty mangled if you passively accept a psychic attack. Let's be honest: If someone jumps you in a parking lot and assaults you, do you really think sending them energy in the form of "warm-fuzzy acceptance, healing, and universal love" will keep you from being any less hurt?

That was a rhetorical question. The answer is obviously *no*.

In reality, you don't send an attacker energy in the hopes that they find peace, healing, and illumination; instead, you channel every bit of your strength so you can fight back and survive. I have always found it interesting that people will go crazy over defending their children or pets; no one even blinks at that. However, everyone goes all up in arms for drawing a hard line at personal psychic self-defense. That makes me ask: What sort of people would do anything to protect their pets or children but then lack the stomach to defend themselves? Martyr, table for one, please.

I do not take a passive sweetness-and-light attitude when it comes to psychic self-defense or to the defense of my person, for that matter. I look at it this way: I will move heaven and earth to avoid a confrontation, but if someone is foolish enough to come after me either energetically or physically with violent intention, then I will do anything and everything in my power to neutralize their attack and stop them cold so they will never even consider it again.

Go ahead, call me a hard-ass. I can take it.

Active, Not Passive:
Tips for Psychic Self-Defense

My philosophy on psychic self-defense may not be what everyone expects from me—you know, married middle-aged mother of three grown kids, living and gardening in the suburbs of the Midwest. *Well gosh, she seemed so funny and nice. Now I'm not so sure. Maybe she's a little scary...* However, before you imagine that folks with a similar mindset to mine are swaggering around, looking for an energetic rumble, keep in mind that we (the psychic self-defense hard-asses of the world) are very aware of the difference between an energetic stumble-and-bump and a purposeful shove or energetic strike. Some folks are simply clumsy with their psychic energy, so keep that in mind.

How do you differentiate? Well, it all comes down to intention and the ferocity of the encounter. Consider this: in the physical world there is a huge difference between an accidental bump and an attacking strike. For example, if someone stumbles and bumps into you in a crowded room, you look around and move back, then check to make sure all of your valuables are where they should be. So while you probably weren't harmed, you are cautious. On the other hand, if someone comes straight at you with their arm raised, then obviously you should move to defend yourself, which should be done as quickly as possible and to the best of your ability. In real life you do not always get the option of avoiding an attack, energetic or otherwise, so being aware of the possibility allows you to consider and plan for how you will best defend yourself with a minimum of fuss in the future.

The practical application of psychic self-defense should be used swiftly and with calm force, which is important. You do not become angry; instead, you channel all of your emotional energy into action and embrace this little thing called emotional neutrality. Getting angry accomplishes nothing. It is a waste of your own personal power. Trust me, once you have experienced an energetic strike or psychic attack, it opens your eyes and makes you rethink psychic self-defense. Throwing anger and hate back at the perpetrator only feeds the attacking energy. Instead, shift your focus, put that energy down, and take it out of the equation. In other words, you neutralize it.

Here are some new and creative ways to go about doing just that.

Psychic Slip

How do you give discordant energy the psychic slip? You dodge it or step out of the line of fire.

> **Psychic Slip:** A term I have adapted from martial arts and boxing terminology. Slipping is defined as smoothly moving out of the way of or dodging an attack. Psychic slipping is also very useful when it comes to dodging another person's inadvertent or clumsy psychic energy so you are not hit or affected by it.

I tend to drop a shoulder when I feel accidental negativity coming my way. Here is how I do it.

PSYCHIC SLIP VERSION ONE

Stand up straight, take a good look around, and open up your psychic abilities. Breathe in and slowly exhale. Count your own heartbeats while you continue those even, smooth breaths and pull in your own personal energy. Now, with a gentle exhale, focus that inner power out a few feet all around yourself. Ask yourself: "What do I see, hear, feel, sense, or know?"

Turn and face the direction where you perceive the clumsy negative energy is coming from. Pull back your personal energy and focus on your own personal power. Take your time; it's not a race. Next, with calm awareness, see the energy coming right at you and then with intention sharply drop your right shoulder, stepping back at the same time with your right foot, and allow the clumsy negative energy to sail right past you.

> **Tips for this maneuver:** Don't pull down at the elbow when you drop your shoulder. Instead, extend your arm down and drop your shoulder; I learned that move in a belly dance class. Visualize that attacking energy blowing smoothly past you and hitting the ground, where it harmlessly dissipates. If you like, you can hold out your dominant hand (the one you write with) and follow up that psychic slip with a gentle push-down movement to give that negative energy a good squash. Once you're done, brush off your hands and walk away confidently, knowing you have just neutralized that attacking energy with a minimum of fuss.

If the shoulder-dropping move eludes you—it does take practice— then try this one instead:

Psychic Slip Version Two

Stand or sit up straight. Now take a good look around and open up your psychic abilities. Breathe in and slowly exhale. Count your own heartbeats while you continue those even and smooth breaths, and pull in your own personal energy. Now with a gentle exhale, focus that inner power out a few feet all around yourself. Ask yourself: "What do I see, hear, feel, sense, or know?"

Turn and face the direction where you perceive that the clumsy negative energy is coming from. Pull your personal energy back and focus on your own personal power. Take your time; it's not a race. Next, with calm awareness see the energy coming right at you and then, with intention, smoothly and sharply turn your body as if you were dodging a playground ball being thrown at you. Remember when you played dodgeball as a kid? This is what we are going for. Quick, smooth, and easy.

Visualize that attacking energy blowing past you and hitting the ground where it harmlessly dissipates. If you like, you can hold out your dominant hand (the one you write with) and follow that up with a gentle push-down movement to give that negative energy a good squash. Once you're done, brush off your hands and move confidently away, knowing you have just neutralized that attacking energy with a minimum of fuss.

Psychic Block

This is not unlike the idea of the psychic shield, but instead of allowing that energy to just bounce off and end up somewhere else, with a psychic block you do not send it back to the instigator. This is not a game of energetic catch. Instead you block and then neutralize any attacking energy by sending the energy to ground, where it can dissolve and be nullified.

> **Psychic Blocking:** Another term that I have adapted from martial arts and boxing terminology. Blocking is the act of stopping or deflecting an opponent's attack, as in deflecting a strike or, in this case, malevolent psychic energy away from both the defender and the attacker.

Psychic Block Directions

Stand up straight and move to an open area. Take a good look around and open up your psychic abilities. Breathe in and slowly exhale. Count your own heartbeats while you continue with those even, smooth breaths and pull in your own personal energy. Now, with a gentle exhale, focus that inner power out a few feet all around yourself. Ask yourself: "What do I see, hear, feel, sense, or know?"

Turn and face the direction where you perceive that the negative energy is coming from. Pull your personal energy back and focus on your own personal power. Take your time; it's not a race. This time you will cross your arms over your chest, making your hands into loose fists.

(Elbows at the waist, fists on the shoulders.) Pull in your power and feel that you are strong and protected. Believe it. You are now blocking any attacking energy. Now, with intention, open your eyes, push your breath out, and swing both arms down, out, and away from the body in one smooth motion. Your arms will now be in an inverted V. Next, you should quickly and with intention crouch down, open your hands, and place your palms on the ground or floor, where the attacking energy will be neutralized by the earth. Take a few deep cleansing breaths and then stand up, brush your hands off, and walk away.

Psychic Parry

To do a psychic parry, we are going to sense the energy and direct it away. Once you have detected it, you calmly manipulate that energy and put it to the ground. Visualize this clearly in your mind. A positive attitude and belief are everything in psychic self-defense.

> **Psychic Parry:** A term I have adapted from fencing and martial arts terminology. A parry is the deflecting or warding off of a thrust or blow. Technically, parries are considered both an evasive and a defensive movement. In martial arts, a parry is executed by quickly pushing an attacker's arm or leg to the side and then counterattacking. A psychic parry involves pushing attacking energy to the side and energetically countering with your own momentum while the opponent is off-balance.

PSYCHIC PARRY DIRECTIONS

Stand up straight, take a good look around, and open up your psychic abilities. Breathe in and slowly exhale. Count your own heartbeats while you continue with those even, smooth breaths and pull in your own personal energy. Now, with a gentle exhale, focus that inner power out a few feet all around yourself. Ask yourself: "What do I see, hear, feel, sense, or know?"

Turn and face the direction where you perceive that the negative energy is coming from. Pull back your personal energy and focus on your own personal power. Take your time; it's not a race.

Hold your hands out at arm's length with the fingers up and palms out. Your hands should be about six inches apart and at heart level. Visualize that encroaching negative energy and feel it against your outstretched hands, then smoothly slide your palms together in front of your heart. Slide both of them together so that your thumbs are touching. Now move the hands together over past your side and to the left. Curve the movement down and bring it back to center, at about hip height. (The beginning of this psychic parry movement is shaped like a backwards question mark.)

Next, take a quick deep breath in, raise your elbows slightly, and picture the attacker being pulled off-balance by the upcoming move. Now firmly push the negative energy down and away from yourself while blowing your breath out with force. Direct that negative energy toward the ground. This is to be a smooth movement. Imagine this as a flowing type of martial arts move if it helps you visualize better. Finally, quickly and with intention, crouch down and place your open palms on the ground or floor, where the attacking energy will be neutralized by the earth. Take a few deep cleansing breaths and then stand up, brush off your hands, and confidently walk away.

The First and Last Line of Defense: It's You!

Practice the psychic slip, block, and parry often. You can choose to perform these psychic self-defense maneuvers subtly or not; it's all up to you. In a pinch I have been known to do these moves with one hand while I was talking to large crowds. Since I always talk with my hands anyway, no one even noticed. Sneaky but effective! As you practice, you will find your own style. It's fun, and if it helps you to get in the mood, put on some music and dance around while you practice. Seriously! Dancing raises positive energy, so get a little going while you practice the psychic slip, block, and parry.

For the individual who is worried about being the target of a psychic attack, let me tell you something very important: people who energetically attack have the mistaken idea that power is something they can take away from another, but that is simply not true. Personal power and psychic ability come from within. They are not exterior forces to be stolen or taken away. When people attack psychically, they do it out of fear. With that thought in mind, I suggest you remember that you already have them running scared, so use that weakness against them.

By practicing psychic self-defense, you are ready to act should the situation ever call for it. At the end of the day, folks who have disciplined both their body and mind make for difficult energetic targets, so be active, not passive, and get to work. You can do this. I have every confidence in you.

THOSE WHO ARE *blessed with*
the most talent don't necessarily
outperform everyone else. It's the people
with follow-through who excel.

Mary Kay Ash

Chapter 9

Where Do You Go from Here?

Where *do* you go from here? Well, my psychic friend, you follow through. You get out there and practice and do your best. Take notes and document your psychic experiences and learn how your own unique psi abilities manifest. Take your time and enjoy the process. I have said that before, and it bears repeating. This is not a contest. You are not expected to outperform other psychics or your friends and family with your superb psychic talents. You are supposed to put your abilities to work and do the best you can.

It is true that some folks may zip right along this personal journey of psychic development with dazzling speed and finesse, and others may prefer to take their time and savor their experiences in a leisurely sort of stroll. However you travel down this path of discovery is up to you. Do not be in a rush. I encourage you to look around and savor the new discoveries you will make along the way.

As we wrap up this book, I want to touch on a few more topics that are going to be important for you while you continue on your journey of psychic development. The first of these is psychic upkeep. Yes, indeed: the general upkeep and care of your personal psychic energy is very important, especially when you are working, exercising, and expanding your own psychic talents. Now that you have an awareness of the psychic realm, you need to become aware of and work on the personal upkeep of your own energetic field.

The Aura: A Rainbow of Colors

An aura is the field of electromagnetic energy that surrounds every living thing. I have purposefully avoided getting into the topic of auras and psychic abilities up until now because folks start to obsess over their own auras and energetic fields. I have seen it happen innumerable times over the years, and honestly it drives me nuts. I have had people rush up and breathlessly ask me to tell them what color their aura is—and then they demand to know what that means. It's always a tossup as to whether I will start to bang my head against the wall in frustration or just give up and laugh until I cry. When it comes to the color of your own aura, the least you need to know is that the color changes constantly. To be honest, the color that is seen or sensed by psychic ability or through an aura camera is only a reflection of your personality, psychic abilities, and current mood. So, everybody: be cool. The aura, with its rainbow of possible colors, is just a beautifully ordinary thing.

For general information purposes, here are the basic meanings of the colors that can be displayed within the human aura. Just remember that your auric field shifts and changes constantly according to your mood.

COLOR	MEANING	PERSONALITY
red	passion, action, ambition	fiery, intense
orange	vibrancy, energy, humor, happiness	fun, outgoing
yellow	radiance, clarity, wisdom	considerate, thoughtful
green	hope, love of nature	nurturing, stable
turquoise	combination of blue and green	inspiring, adventurous
blue	psychic ability, sensitivity	loving, kind
violet	strong psychic power, fantasy, spirituality	mystical, powerful
pink	romance, love, buoyancy	gentle, loving
white	connection to the Divine, spirituality, peace	calm, wise

It may also interest you to know that your auric energy pattern—which manifests as a color—can also be manipulated and changed on command by your own will. No kidding. I have proven that theory by sitting at a friend's aura photography machine and focusing on changing my aura color on purpose. We turned the computer monitor toward me, and I asked everyone present to watch the screen with me while I explained my theory that the colors of your personal energy field could be manipulated at will. I announced I was going to change my color of orange, which was currently displayed, to blue and green. It was a riot to watch the expressions on people's faces while the computer monitor showed the aura colors around me quickly shifting to those chosen cooler colors of blue and green.

Then another person decided they wanted to try it, so I encouraged her to wait and see what her first color readout was. While the computer picked up her energy field and displayed one set of colors, I suggested that she focus on violet and pink and think about love and spirituality—hard. Sure enough, the colors shifted immediately over to rosy pink and a pretty amethyst. So before you get all fixated on your aura color and what it can mean, remember that it is only a reflection of what you are currently experiencing on an emotional and spiritual level. The fact that the aura can be changed by focusing your intent and will upon it is a perfect illustration of mind over matter.

Auric Upkeep: Psychic Hygiene

Realizing that your aura color and pattern can be shifted and directed at your will, let's take this to the next logical step, shall we? Your aura is a ever-evolving reflection of your personality, mood, and also your own psychic abilities. That being said, it can also pick up psychic debris and energetic gunk without your being aware of it. The best way I have seen this described is that it's not unusual to go through your day without noticing a stain on your favorite shirt or a scuff on your new shoes. It always gives you a jolt to realize that stain or scuff was there all day long, and you were blissfully unaware of it.

The same can be said for stains, scuffs, or tears in the auric field. We can unintentionally pick up on negative psychic or emotional energy from other people or places. This leaves a worn-down area. (This is typically a minor problem, so stay with me here.)

The truth of the matter is that as you have developed your psychic talents, you have also developed an awareness of, and interacted with, the subtle energies of other people and places that are all around you. You should regularly check your personal energetic field, or your own aura, by looking for anything amiss.

How will you know? Auric colors tend to be bright and vibrant shades. If for some reason the shades of your aura seem discolored, muddy, or dull, or you can feel by running your hands over your own energy field that you have blank or cold spots, then this is a signal to you that you have some weak spots or tears in your personal energetic field. (Pass your open hands over and about six inches away from your own body to sense this for yourself.) Depending on your own psi abilities, you may feel the tears, see them in your mind's eye, have sudden cognitive pops of information as to where the problem is, or be listening to your inner monologue and discovering what you hear.

It is also important to know that if you overextend yourself with the use of your psychic abilities (aka a psychic hangover), a weakening of the auric field can also happen. The only time these scruffs, stains, and tears become a problem is when you ignore them for long periods of time. Being oblivious to your auric upkeep can affect your physical well-being. The next thing you know, you are constantly sick or experiencing an overwhelming case of the blahs.

It is when we do finally notice these little tears in our own energetic field that we wonder how in the hell we ever overlooked them in the first place. That's okay—you will bounce back quickly enough. Being aware is half of the battle. However, now that you have figured it out, it is time to act and do a little cleansing, repair, and general maintenance of the auric field. Here is how you go about doing just that.

Washing

The fastest way to get the auric repair process started is to take a shower. Yeah, you heard me—hit the showers! The age-old cure of running water is a potent one. This is not unlike the fourth step in psychic first aid; however, this time you will need to visualize that as the water pours over your head and then down the rest of you, it is washing away any lingering negativity or imperfections in your personal energy field. Sitting in a bathtub full of water and soaking just won't cut it for aura repair and upkeep. You need to wash those imperfections off and away. If you only have a tub, then I suggest you get a big pitcher of warm water, strip down, stand in the bathtub, and pour the whole business over your head with the intention that as the water runs down your body, it washes away any psychic residue and seals any scuffs or tears in your aura. If you perform this simple act with intention, it can and will become a powerful act of psychic upkeep.

Smudging

This is a quick and pleasant way to clear negative energy from a person or place by waving incense smoke around the area or over a person. Smudging works with the element of air and is a time-honored way of energetic cleansing. Some folks like to use bundles of white sage for smudging, but I actually prefer sandalwood incense sticks. Sage makes me sneeze violently, and it sort of kills the cleansing mood if the scent you are using makes you sneeze and wheeze. Sandalwood is clean, light, and readily available; it is thought to be a highly spiritual scent.

Start at the top of your head and carefully wave some of the scented smoke over your head and down your trunk. Move down to the legs. Hold your arms out and let them pass through the smoke as well. To do your back, hold the incense at waist level in one spot for a moment. Let a bit of smoke gather, then turn around and back through it or you can have someone else fan the scented smoke over you. Please be careful and watch for falling ash when you smudge. I recommend keeping the stick in an incense holder that is designed to catch that falling ash.

Mending

Mending tears in your aura is a simple process that requires a bit of imagination and visualization on your part. To start, you have to be able to locate any thin spots or tears in your own aura, as was suggested earlier. Once you have located the thin spots or tears, then you take both of your hands and smooth the edges of your own aura back in place and then "sew" them together. I suggest taking the first finger of your dominant hand and then bending it slightly, visualizing that your finger is now like a curved needle. Now, with a looping gesture and intention, pantomime that you are stitching those open edges of your aura back together. Then, once that is done, hold your hands out and sense that the area is now mended. Seal it with a bright bolt of your own personal energy: use your dominant hand and visualize colorful energy shooting out and sealing up the area. I suggest that you pick a happy color for this. Personally I like hot pink or turquoise for sealing up any mending to the aura, but follow your instincts and see what you decide will be the most complementary healing color for you to use. (Refer to the aura color chart earlier in this chapter.)

Finally, to help put your energies back on track or heal any auric issues, consider working a simple, beautiful ceremony after washing, smudging, or mending. I have found that ceremonies help our minds to switch over from the everyday to the miraculous. The following rite will assist you with energetic repairs to your aura.

Ceremony for Repairing the Aura

To begin, you are going to want to choose a few bright, happy colors that you intuitively find to be healing colors for you. Some folks insist that white light is the only way to go, but I have found over the years that working with whatever vibrant color or colors you intuitively choose gives you much better results. Take a look at that aura chart again, and see which color or colors you are drawn to. Follow your hunches; they won't lead you astray. Be creative and use your intuition! Find and follow your own truth. After all, no two people are the same, and making your ceremony personal is what gives it punch and power.

Timing: I would perform this healing ceremony at sunrise or sunset. These are powerful times of the day: there is wonder at the opening of a day and mystery at the beginning of night. This is natural energy, and it is complementary to any personal spiritual path.

Supplies: Yourself and your own intention to create a positive change.

Directions: Stand with your feet comfortably apart. Take a few moments to slow down your breathing and wait until you can hear your own breath and the beating of your heart. Then say out loud:

> *In this sacred time and in this hour*
> *I call upon my own healing powers.*

Now turn your hands palms up and lift them out to your sides at waist level. Visualize a healing color or colors of your own choosing hovering at your fingertips and waiting for your command. Continue with:

> *As I lift my hands, I raise up my own energy*
> *Now I'll send it spinning around to encircle me.*

With a smooth gesture, turn your hands over so both palms are turned to the right, then gently and smoothly "push" that healing energy and color off to your right and send it spinning around yourself clockwise. After you have pushed the energy around, then gently lower your hands to your sides and visualize your own innate healing powers spinning around you with a happy hum of energy and in bright and glowing healing colors. Then say:

> *With this action, tears or stains in my aura will mend*
> *Leaving me calm, refreshed, happy, and whole once again.*

Stay put for as long as you'd like. After a few moments the spinning energy will dissipate. Pay attention; you will feel it wane. Close your eyes and use those psychic abilities you have been developing. You may just know, hear, feel, or see with your inner eye when the circling energy has waned. Now you can close up your healing ceremony. Raise your hands up so your palms face together in a prayer position. Hold your hands loosely pressed together and at heart height. Take a nice deep breath in through your nose and hold your breath for four counts, then slowly blow out your breath through your mouth. Close the ceremony with these lines:

Surrounded by healing color(s) so bright
I close this work with gratitude and light.

Let your hands drop to your sides and relax. Now go about the rest of your day and enjoy yourself.

Complementary Crystals for Psychic Work

Over the years I have found that working with tumbled stones and various crystals is a smart way to enhance my psychic work. I have successfully employed crystals to enhance my psychic talents, and I have also used crystals to aid in psychic protection, auric cleansing, and auric healing. There is a wealth of power in the earth and the stones, gems, and crystals that come from it.

Here is a quick list of some of my favorite crystals and stones for psychic work. The majority of these featured crystals are easy to find—just check your local metaphysical store and peruse their selection of tumbled stones. I recommend that you clear your new crystals after you purchase them. Also, if you have had crystals or tumbled stones in your possession for a while, the same thing goes.

Clearing Crystals and Stones

The easiest way to clear energies from your crystals and stones is to set them on a windowsill so they can absorb sunlight or the light of a full moon. This is a time-honored and natural way to cleanse crystals and stones. On the night of the full moon each and every month, I set my dish of tumbled stones and crystals on the inside windowsill that faces east. I leave the dish in place until sunrise, and that way the crystals have received both moonlight and sunlight and are cleansed and ready to go for whatever purposes I will need them for.

The following is a list of crystals and stones that will be beneficial for you to employ as you work on your own psychic development.

> **Amethyst:** This gorgeous purple gemstone is a powerful and protective crystal. It is believed to protect its wearer from psychic attack and is a calming, stress-relieving stone that is good for mediums to work with. I recommend a piece of jewelry that you always wear for this purpose. The amethyst also promotes claircognizance and clairvoyance, plus it helps to bring mind, body, and spirit into balance.

> **Apatite:** This is an easily obtained multi-hued crystal most often found in yellow to olive-green shades. It is also available in deep blue, which is popular in jewelry. A good stone to work with as you begin to develop your psychic talents, it also enhances clairvoyance, clairaudience, and clairsentience.

> **Aquamarine:** The aquamarine gemstone is fabulous for the psychic sensitive. It is classically used to sharpen clairvoyant abilities and is rumored to help mediums make a clearer connection the other side. Look for low-grade tumbled stones or finer specimens at gem and mineral shows. You could also invest in a piece of aquamarine jewelry.

Black Tourmaline: One of the best stones for psychic protection from others' negative psychic energy. An incredibly powerful stone for protection work on all levels. If you feel particularly under the effect of other people's psychic influences, set black tourmaline on your nightstand while you sleep.

Bloodstone: This is a deep green stone with flecks of red bleeding through. Bloodstones are used for healing work, as they promote both physical and psychic health. An excellent stone to work with if you need to recoup and recharge after a psychic overextension or for repairing tears or scuffs in your aura.

Labradorite: This blue-gray stone is used for transformation and for clear seeing. This crystal promotes clairvoyance, banishes fear and anxiety, and can help remove psychic gunk from your aura.

Lapis Lazuli: This dark blue stone is flecked with gold. Called the seer's stone and known for opening up psychic vision (clairvoyance), it is also excellent for repelling psychic attacks. This stone helps restore a healthy emotional balance.

Lavender Quartz: A variety of rose quartz that is a soft opaque lavender color. It promotes clairaudience, clairvoyance, and clairsentience, and it bestows an extra boost of energy. A very loving, comforting stone, it's well worth the search to acquire one.

Moonstone: Moonstones are wonderful crystals to help open up your sensitivity to others. Used as a talisman for safe travel, this receptive and calming crystal heightens all psychic abilities, especially intuition, clairtangency, clairvoyance, and clairsentience. Moonstone would also help a psychic sensitive get a better read for locations and local ghosts, as this crystal opens up your ability to receive impressions.

Onyx: This stone is all about memories, which makes it a useful tool for postcognitive experiences, as well as for aiding the psychic ability of clairtangency and the art of psychometry. Onyx is also a very potent protection from psychic attack.

Quartz Crystal (Clear): This is a power stone, plain and simple. Quart crystal points act as clarifiers, power generators, and batteries for the times when you need a little extra "juice," or energy. I like to keep a small crystal point with my tarot cards to add a little extra clarity to my readings.

Rhodocrosite: A beautiful banded stone in shades of pink with white, gray, and black. This is a stone of love and compassion. Rhodocrosite helps us learn from past mistakes and keeps our heart open. This stone is excellent for when you are healing from a psychic overextension.

Smoky Quartz: Smoky quartz is a gorgeous smoky-brown variety of quartz crystal. It neutralizes negative emotions and energies, plus it pulls positive energies into a space. This would be a fine stone to wear or carry while working psychic self-defense.

Tiger's-Eye: The golden-brown banded tiger's-eye stone is an energy-boosting, courageous stone, excellent for use in psychic self-defense. Tiger's-eye will ward off jealous feelings from your detractors, as well as help you to stay grounded and complete your goals.

Turquoise: Well known for its healing and emotionally protective properties, turquoise is an aid for claircognizance. Turquoise is also a purification stone, and it bestows tranquility on its wearer.

Now stop and consider which of these crystals would complement the various psychic abilities and techniques that you have read about throughout this book. Imagine tucking onyx or black tourmaline in your pocket while you work on psychic self-defense, or adding a chunk of quartz crystal or amethyst to your table as you work with tarot cards. Tiger's-eye would be most beneficial to removing blocks as you expand your psychic skills. Try adding labradorite, rhodocrosite, or bloodstone to auric upkeep and repairs…the possibilities are endless. Be creative; see what you can come up with!

Finally, check out this quick list of complementary crystals for specific psychic abilities and needs.

Complementary Crystals for Specific Psychic Uses

To promote clairaudience (psychic hearing): apatite, lavender quartz

To promote claircognizance (psychic intuition): amethyst, moonstone, turquoise

To promote clairsentience (psychic empathy): apatite, lavender quartz, moonstone

To promote clairtangency (psychic touch): moonstone, onyx

To promote clairvoyance (psychic seeing): amethyst, apatite, aquamarine, labradorite, lavender quartz, lapis lazuli, moonstone

To assist with mediumship: amethyst, aquamarine

To assist the psychic sensitive: aquamarine, moonstone

To promote psychic self-defense: black tourmaline, lapis lazuli, onyx, smoky quartz, tiger's-eye

To promote auric repair and cleansing: amethyst, bloodstone, labradorite, turquoise

To help recover after psychic overextension: bloodstone, rhodocrosite

Focus on the journey, not the destination. Joy is found not in finishing an activity but in doing it.

Greg Anderson

Closing Thoughts

I hope that you have enjoyed your time spent with me while we have worked on your personal psychic development. Know that you are not finished with this journey; instead, you are merely at a crossroads. Now the choice is up to you as to where you will go next and what lessons you will choose to take with you. Once you begin this path of personal expansion and have opened up your mind to the possibilities of your own natural psychic abilities and experiences, you will never look at the world in the same way again—and that is a very good thing.

Your own unique horizons have been broadened, and your options are now more wonderful and varied than ever before. Now the challenge that faces you is this: each and every day you should actively seek out a new way in which to use your psychic abilities. Find ways to practice, improve, and fine-tune your skills. Remember to be considerate and thoughtful when you share any gained psychic information with others, for it is vital to behave ethically and compassionately.

At the end of the day, my best hope for your own future is that you will listen to your intuition, pay attention to the messages that your psychic abilities are telling you, follow your heart, and then live your life in the best way that you possibly can.

By exploring your own natural psychic experiences and talents, you have enriched your life and expanded your world. Take a deep breath and look around you. The future is bright! Now go forward with confidence in your psychic abilities, and enjoy the journey.

Words do two things: they provide
food for the mind and create light for
understanding and awareness.

Jim Rohn

Glossary

Aura: The field of electromagnetic energy that surrounds every living thing. The aura's color constantly shifts and is an expression of your personality and mood.

Clairaudience or Telepathy: The ability to receive extrasensory signals as a word, sound, or song. A clairaudient picks up words, sounds, music, or tones that are not discernible to the average ear. Also, a clairaudient gathers psychic information from listening to their own inner monologue. Classically, telepathy is defined as the transmission of unspoken thoughts or psychic impressions from one person to another. Simply put, a clairaudient/telepath hears their psychic information.

Claircognizance (Psychic Intuition): A psychic intuitive is an individual who has an immediate insight or cognition. Claircognizance means "clear knowing." Claircognizance/intuition is one of the most common ESP abilities. This ability is sometimes called "prophetic knowing." As that good old-fashioned "gut hunch," that instantaneous awareness, it truly is an extrasensory knowing.

Clairsentience (Psychic Empathy): Defined as "clear feeling." The clairsentient, or empath, can sense and obtain psychic information through the energies, feelings, and emotions of those who are around them or in their general vicinity. A psychic empath/clairsentient is a person who can physically tune into the emotional experiences of another person or a place. They sense attitudes, emotions, and sometimes physical ailments.

Clairtangency (Psychometry): Defined as "clear touching." With clairtangency, psychic information is gathered by the physical touch of the hands. If you touch someone—say, as in a handshake—and receive psychic information, this is the act of psychometry and you are, in fact, employing the psychic ability of clairtangency. The ability of clairtangency can be experienced as either a precognitive or postcognitive event.

Clairvoyance: The ability to perceive things that cannot be seen with the physical eye; instead, they are seen internally. Clairvoyants can see images and pictures that may be symbolic or as intense and detailed as watching a miniature psychic movie scene inside your mind. Clairvoyants can literally see the past (postcognition), the present, and the future (precognition).

Déjà vu: French for "already seen," this is when an event occurs and you have the sensation of repeating something that has already been experienced, seen, or felt. This memory from your own future, while familiar to you, still feels very strange. The déjà vu sensation jolts typically you into remembering your previous precognitive dream or temporarily forgotten precognitive experience.

Energy Vampires: Psychic or emotional vampires are individuals who drain or leech the energy, good mood, and vitality from another person. A psi-vamp or emo-vamp may be unaware and accidental or unrepentant and uninvited.

Ghost: A noncorporeal presence that manifests or remains in the physical world.

Gut Hunch: A gut hunch is a way to get your attention as the precognitive information rolls through. When a gut hunch occurs, the psychic information is simultaneous: the information and the physical sensation occur in your belly at the same time. Associated with claircognizance/intuition.

Hunch: An unexpected sense of a future event or outcome. (*see* Gut Hunch)

Major Arcana Cards: The scenes in the twenty-two major arcana tarot cards show us evocative images and archetypes. These archetypes are symbolic figures such as the Traveler or the Seeker, the Mother, the Father, the High Priest, the High Priestess, and the Hero. They appear in various mythologies, religions, and mystery traditions from all over the world.

These twenty-two cards appeal to our emotions and tug on our heartstrings. The imagery and archetypes within the major arcana link us all together because they resonate on a deeper spiritual level. When major arcana cards turn up in a tarot spread, they add weight and importance to the reading. These cards illustrate important spiritual matters and reveal our relationship to the particular archetype within the major arcana card.

Medium: A person who acts as a bridge (mediates) between the world of spirit and the living. A medium is tuned into the other side—the realm of spirit—and can communicate with presences in that world. Mediumship is a form of psychic communication. (*see* chapter 4)

Minor Arcana Cards: The minor arcana consists of four different suits: cups, swords, wands, and pentacles. Each of these suits aligns with one of the four natural elements. The different elements characterize not only different experiences but also very different ways of approaching the challenges in your life. Also, within each of the four suits there are two different sets of cards: the pips, or numbered cards (the ace through ten), and the court cards (the page, knight, queen, and king). The court cards classically represent the real people and personalities whom you have to interact with in your life.

Overextension: Going beyond your physical or psychic abilities into the realm of strain or injury. Also called a psychic hangover.

Paranormal: Beyond the range of scientifically known phenomena.

Power Animal: Also called an animal ally or animal totem. Many different cultures work with animal spirits for guidance and protection during spiritual journeys. A power animal tends to be an animal that you are attracted to. The particular strengths and attributes of that animal create a connection and a natural empowering energy between the two of you.

Precognition: Also sometimes referred to as precog, it is the direct knowledge of events that have yet to occur. Precognition may be experienced in the dream state (as in precognitive dreams) or it can also be readily experienced as a waking vision. Precognition is very specific psychic information without any emotional reaction at the time the knowledge is received. Precognitive information may be received by means of psychic touching (clairtangency), psychic hearing (clairaudience), psychic knowing (intuition), psychic empathy (clairsentience), or a psychic vision (clairvoyance).

Premonition: An unclear forewarning accompanied by a simultaneous emotional reaction. This vague feeling of unease that something is wrong can be hard to pin down or put a name on. With a premonition, you feel a sense of danger, urgency, or apprehension, but you do not receive any specific information; instead, this is all about that emotional feeling.

Postcognition: Sometimes called retrocognition, it is the experience of receiving extrasensory images or impressions from the past. A postcognitive episode may be experienced by means of psychic touching (clairtangency), psychic hearing (clairaudience), psychic knowing (intuition), psychic empathy (clairsentience), or a psychic vision (clairvoyance).

Presence: I typically refer to the people or personalities I encounter from the other side while performing mediumship readings as presences. I do this to differentiate between a ghost or spirit that is bound to the physical plane. Those presences I connect with during a medium-style reading are not here on the earthly plane, as a medium can only communicate with them while they remain on the other side. A medium works as a bridge from our physical plane to the other side.

Psi: Short for psychic. Occasionally you may see this as psi-ability (psychic ability), psi-experiences (psychic experiences), psi-sensitive (psychic sensitive), or psi-vamp (psychic vampire).

Psi-Sensitive (Psychic Sensitive): A person who has psychic sensitivity picks up more emotional information about their environment and the people around them than the average person. Typically a psi-sensitive has an extremely fine-tuned ability of clairsentience, or psychic empathy.

Psychic: A person who is sensitive to nonphysical forces and influences. They obtain knowledge from outside the realm of the physical senses.

Psychic Ability: An individual's capability to receive information in a way that is beyond the nonphysical senses. This natural skill, or aptitude, is considered extra—as in extrasensory perception, or ESP for short.

Psychic Attack: The unconscious or purposeful focusing of psychic or mental energies to bring emotional harm to another individual.

Psychic Blocking: A term I have adapted from martial arts and boxing terminology. Blocking is the act of stopping or deflecting an opponent's attack, as in deflecting a strike—or, in this case, malevolent psychic energy away from both the defender and the attacker.

Psychic Experience: The process of personally experiencing or having a premonition, precognition, or postcognition.

Psychic Hangover: The backlash from doing too much psychic work. As an energetic sort of hangover, this overextension can also combine with physical symptoms.

Psychic Parry: A term I have adapted from fencing and martial arts terminology. A parry is the deflecting or warding off of a thrust or blow. Technically, parries are considered both an evasive and a defensive movement. In martial arts, a parry is executed by quickly pushing an attacker's arm or leg to the side and then counterattacking, so a psychic parry involves pushing attacking energy to the side and energetically countering with your own momentum while the opponent is off balance.

Psychic Ping: What I call the instantaneous awareness of intuition: a sudden cognitive pop of psychic information.

Psychic Self-Defense: The act of defending yourself from another's negative psychic energy or depressing thoughts. A way to protect yourself from being emotionally vulnerable to the barbs, digs, and mind games from everyday life. Think of psychic self-defense as a little extra insulation from the jealous, emotionally draining, or unhappy people we all encounter. (*see* chapter 8)

Psychic Slip: A term I have adapted from martial arts and boxing terminology. Slipping is defined as smoothly moving out of the way, or dodging an attack and not being hit.

Psychometry: The reading of an object or person using the psychic ability of clairtangency, or psychic touch. Psychometry readings tend to be mainly postcognitive experiences.

R&R: This stands for "recoup and recharge" and refers to the act of recouping lost personal energy and recharging your physical body.

Remote Viewing: Using the mind to view a person, place, or object that is located a distance away, beyond the physical realm of sight. Basically it is using clairvoyant ability in the present.

Residual Haunt: One of the most common types of hauntings. A person with postcognitive abilities can pick up on the memories or traumatic events and keep sensing the emotional imprint these events have left behind.

Séance: A gathering of people for the purpose of attempting spirit communication.

Sensitive: A person who is able to sense when a ghost or spirit is nearby on the earthly, or physical, plane. They might physically hear, see, or feel the manifestation of a ghost.

SLIder: An acronym that stands for Street Lamp Interference Data Exchange Receiver. SLI phenomena is a type of psychic experience. (*see* chapter 6)

SLI Experiences: Psychic experiences that typically involve the unexplained malfunction of electronic devices or the blowing out of light bulbs and street lamps around a specific individual on a regular basis. (*see* chapter 6)

Smudging: A way to clear negative energy from a person or place by waving incense smoke around the area or over a person. Smudging works with the element of air and is a time-honored way of energetic cleansing.

Spirit Guide: A spirit guide is an archetypal representation of a spiritual path or personal lesson. Spirit guides tend manifest as classic archetypes such as Teacher, Wise Woman, Sage, Warrior, Hero, or Healer. A spirit guide is always benevolent, supportive, and sometimes humorous. Spirit guides can provide answers or insights to dreams and your own personal path. They may make themselves known to you as a recurring character in your dreams or during meditation. You can have more than one spirit guide during your life, and they sometimes come and go as they are needed.

Tarot Card Spreads: Spreads are the patterns that tarot cards are laid out in, which provides the structure for any tarot reading. In this book you will find instructions for one-card, three-card, and seven-card tarot spreads. (*see* chapter 5)

Tarot Deck: A deck of seventy-eight mystical cards that has been used for centuries as a divinatory tool. A tarot deck is classically made up of twenty-two major arcana cards and fifty-six minor arcana cards, which are divided into the four suits of cups, wands, swords, and pentacles.

Third Eye: The seat of a clairvoyant's power, the third eye is located in the center of the forehead.

WRITE TO BE *understood, speak to be heard, read to grow.*

Lawrence Clark Powell

Bibliography

Alvarez, Melissa. *Your Psychic Self.* Woodbury, MN: Llewellyn, 2013.

Andrews, Ted. *How to Develop and Use Psychometry.* St. Paul, MN: Llewellyn, 1994.

Bartlett, Sarah. *The Essential Guide to Psychic Powers.* London: Watkins, 2012.

Belanger, Michelle. *The Psychic Energy Codex.* San Francisco, CA: Weiser Books, 2007.

Burns, Litany. *Develop Your Psychic Abilities.* New York: Pocket Books, 1987.

Cuhulain, Kerr. *Magickal Self Defense.* Woodbury, MN: Llewellyn, 2008.

Donnelly, Katherine Fair. *The Guidebook to ESP and Psychic Wonders.* New York: David McKay Company, Inc., 1978.

Dugan, Ellen. *Natural Witchery.* Woodbury, MN: Llewellyn, 2007.

———. *Practical Protection Magick.* Woodbury, MN: Llewellyn, 2011.

———. *Witches Tarot Companion.* Woodbury, MN: Llewellyn, 2012.

Edward, John. *Infinite Quest.* New York: Sterling, 2010.

Gallagher, Anne-Marie. *Magical Spells for Your Home.* Hauppauge, NY: Barron's, 2002.

Grant, Ember. *The Book of Crystal Spells.* Woodbury, MN: Llewellyn, 2013.

Hall, Judy. *The Crystal Bible.* Cincinnati, OH: Walking Stick Press, 2003.

———. *Psychic Protection.* London: Thorsons, 1999.

Johnson, Julie Tallard. *Teen Psychic.* Rochester, VT: Bindu Books, 2003.

Melody. *Love Is in the Earth: A Kaleidoscope of Crystals.* Wheat Ridge, CO: Earth-Love Publishing House, 1995.

Moore, Barbara. *Tarot for Beginners.* Woodbury, MN: Llewellyn, 2010.

Moorey, Teresa. *Working with Psychic Protection.* New York: Sterling, 2007.

Naiman, Carolyn. "The Clairsentient Psychic," from http://EzineArticles.com/?The-Clairsentient-Psychic&id=4281991.

Naparstek, Belleruth. *Your Sixth Sense: Activating Your Psychic Potential.* San Francisco, CA: Harper Collins, 1997.

O'Neill, Jennifer. *Intuition & Psychic Ability.* Kailua, HI: Limitless Publishing, 2012.

Penczak, Christopher. *The Inner Temple of Witchcraft*. St. Paul, MN: Llewellyn, 2003.

Powell, Diane Hennacy. *The ESP Enigma*. New York: Walker, 2009.

Robinson, Lynn A., and LaVonne Carlson-Finnerty. *The Complete Idiot's Guide to Being Psychic*. Indianapolis, IN: Alpha Books, 1999.

Sanders, Pete A. *You Are Psychic!* New York: Ballantine Books, 1990.

Silva, Jose Jr., and Ed Bernd Jr. *Jose Silva's Everyday ESP*. Pompton Plains, NJ: New Page Books, 2007.

Soskin, Julie. *How Psychic Are You?* New York: Penguin Books, 2002.

Whitehurst, Tess. *Magical Housekeeping*. Woodbury, MN: Llewellyn, 2010.

———. *The Good Energy Book*. Woodbury, MN: Llewellyn, 2011.

PREDICTING THE FUTURE *is easy.*
It's trying to figure out what is
going on now that is hard.

Fritz R. S. Dressler

Index

Garden Witchery
Magick from the Ground Up
Ellen Dugan

How does your magickal garden grow? *Garden Witchery* is more than belladonna and wolfsbane. It's about making your own enchanted backyard with the trees, flowers, and plants found growing around you. It's about creating your own flower fascinations and spells, and it's full of common-sense information about cold hardiness zones, soil requirements, and a realistic listing of accessible magickal plants.

There may be other books on magickal gardening, but none have practical gardening advice, magickal correspondences, flower folklore, moon gardening, faery magick, advanced Witchcraft, and humorous personal anecdotes all rolled into one volume. *Garden Witchery* is now available in a tenth anniversary edition. Includes a gardening journal.

978-0-7387-0318-3
7½ x 7½ • 304 pp.

To order, call 1-877-NEW-WRLD

Prices subject to change without notice

Order at llewellyn.com 24 hours a day, 7 days a week!

Cottage Witchery
Natural Magick for Hearth and Home
Ellen Dugan

There's no place like a magickal home—and Ellen Dugan, the author of *Garden Witchery*, is the ideal guide to show us how to bring the beauty of nature and its magickal energies indoors. Using common household and outdoor items—such as herbs, spices, dried flowers, plants, stones, and candles—she offers a down-to-earth approach to creating an enchanted home.

From specialized spells and charms to kitchen conjuring and color magick, this hands-on guide teaches Witches of all levels how to strengthen a home's aura and energy. Readers will learn how to use begonias and lilacs for protection, dispel bad vibes with salt and lemon, perform tea leaf readings, bless the home with fruit, invite the help of faeries, perform houseplant magick, and create a loving home for the whole family.

978-0-7387-0625-2
7½ x 7½ • 288 pp.

To order, call 1-877-NEW-WRLD

Prices subject to change without notice

Order at llewellyn.com 24 hours a day, 7 days a week!

Seasons of Witchery
*Celebrating the Sabbats
with the Garden Witch*

Ellen Dugan

In *Seasons of Witchery*, the newest release in Ellen Dugan's best-selling series, she offers readers a wealth of magickal ways to celebrate the wheel of the year. With her trademark warmth and practicality, Ellen shares a bit of history and lore on each sabbat as well as simple yet meaningful ideas for honoring each season. There are colorful decorating suggestions, fun craft projects, tasty recipes, insightful journal notes about her enchanted garden through the year, and natural magick aligned with each holiday. This charming and friendly book will inspire readers with new ideas, fresh spells, and seasonal rituals to make their own sabbat celebrations more personal and powerful.

978-0-7387-3078-3
7½ x 7½ • 336 pp.

To order, call 1-877-NEW-WRLD

Prices subject to change without notice

Order at llewellyn.com 24 hours a day, 7 days a week!

Book of Witchery
Spells, Charms & Correspondences
for Every Day of the Week
Ellen Dugan

Kick-start your magickal creativity and incorporate the Craft into your everyday life. Award-winning author Ellen Dugan offers many fresh ideas on building your own personal style of witchery, so you can happily conjure seven days a week. This friendly guide will help you learn the fundamentals and make good use of the magickal energies each day holds. Formerly available as *7 Days of Magic*, this treasury of Witchcraft essentials has more than doubled in size and features a wealth of brand-new material.

978-0-7387-1584-1
7½ x 7½ • 360 pp.

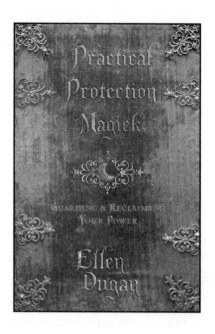

To order, call 1-877-NEW-WRLD

Prices subject to change without notice

Order at llewellyn.com 24 hours a day, 7 days a week!

Practical Protection Magick
Guarding & Reclaiming Your Power

Ellen Dugan

Embrace your inner warrior to safeguard your personal power. Use protection magick and psychic self-defense to stay strong, healthy, and happy.

With honesty and humor, best-selling author Ellen Dugan teaches how to weave safe and sensible protection magick into your practice and daily life. This unique practical guide reveals how to pinpoint your psychic strengths, set boundaries, diagnose a problem with divination, and maintain health on physical, psychic, and magickal levels. You'll also find simple and potent spells, rituals, and warding techniques to defend against psychic attacks, emotional and psychic vampires, hexes, unwanted ghosts, and other forms of negativity threatening your home and your well-being.

978-0-7387-2168-2
6 x 9, 240 pp.

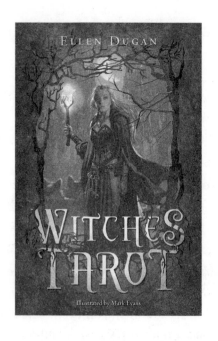

To order, call 1-877-NEW-WRLD

Prices subject to change without notice

Order at llewellyn.com 24 hours a day, 7 days a week!

Witches Tarot
Illustrated by Mark Evans

Ellen Dugan

Witches the world over will relish this new tarot! Award-winning author Ellen Dugan, a highly respected Witch and tarot reader, and award-winning artist Mark Evans have created the perfect deck for all devotees of the Craft.

Positively radiating witchy energy, this easy-to-use tarot showcases beautiful and evocative digital artwork. Echoing the traditional Rider-Waite structure, each card includes instantly recognizable Pagan symbols that resonate with today's Witch. In addition to card descriptions and meanings, Dugan's companion guide features seven unique, spell-enhancing spreads for both tarot readings and magickal practice.

978-0-7387-2800-1
kit includes 312-pp. book and 78-card deck

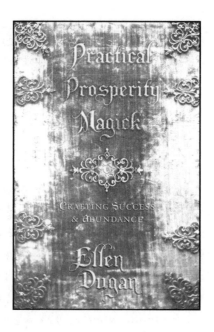

To order, call 1-877-NEW-WRLD

Prices subject to change without notice

Order at llewellyn.com 24 hours a day, 7 days a week!

Practical Prosperity Magick
Crafting Success & Abundance
Ellen Dugan

Financial prosperity is within reach for everyone. Let Ellen Dugan show you how to work magick to achieve abundance and transform bad luck to good luck. Filled with humor and no-nonsense advice, *Practical Prosperity Magick* features spells, charms, and rituals for creating wealth; tips for working with the law of attraction; how-to instructions for herbs and crystals; good-luck charms and talismans; and techniques for solitary and group rituals.

Break down the blocks that have kept you from achieving your goals. Using the four elements as the foundations for prosperity, this down-to-earth guide explores the seven Hermetic laws and planetary techniques to help you stay upbeat and draw money quickly. Ellen Dugan's user-friendly style makes prosperity magick safe, practical, and easy—and above all, it works.

978-0-7387-3696-9

6 x 9, 264 pp.

To Write to the Author

If you wish to contact the author or would like more information about this book, please write to the author in care of Llewellyn Worldwide and we will forward your request. Both the author and the publisher appreciate hearing from you and learning of your enjoyment of this book and how it has helped you. Llewellyn Worldwide cannot guarantee that every letter written to the author can be answered, but all will be forwarded. Please write to:

Ellen Dugan
℅ Llewellyn Worldwide
2143 Wooddale Drive
Woodbury, MN 55125-2989

Please enclose a self-addressed stamped envelope for reply
or $1.00 to cover costs. If outside the USA, enclose
an international postal reply coupon.

Many of Llewellyn's authors have websites with additional information and resources. For more information, please visit our website:

WWW.LLEWELLYN.COM